Nigerians' Views on National Turmoil

A Situational Quadruple Nexus Analysis

Babafemi A. Badejo

YINTAB BOOKS

LAGOS | 2022

Yintab Books, a division of Yintab Ltd.

Yintab Compound

TOS Benson Estate Road, Oja Bus Stop

Ikorodu, Lagos, Nigeria

www.yintabstrategyconsults.com

ISBN

978-978-998-0413 | Paperback

978-978-998-2080 | E-book

Table of Contents

Chapter Three

Chapter Four

Acknowledgements

In many respects, this volume would not have seen the light of day without the many collaborations I have enjoyed from my getting to know Johnstone Oketch Summit (JOS). Aside from throwing my CV into the kitty during an ECA search for a Consultant on Four-Pillar Interlinkages for West and Central Africa, JOS has always found time to listen to me and engage me with a lot of intellect during several brainstorming sessions. My agitations on the situational foundations (governance, external dynamics, institutions and resources) of conflicts, underdevelopment, violations of human rights, and failures on humanitarian affairs in Africa received a lot of understanding and desire to help build from JOS. This debate continued as the UN Economic Commission for Africa (UNECA) proactively and rightly pushed for four-pillar interlinkages for operational purposes as an improvement on the three-pillar interlinkages (Triple Nexus).

I owe a lot to the UNECA Team on the four-pillar interlinkages project led by Ms. Isatou Gaye. The constant interactions with them on the Terms of Reference as well as on the report on West and Central Africa was a major spur for my developing the idea further. Other Independent Consultants on the ECA project, including Prof. Thokozani Kaime; Prof. Stephen Commins; Prof. Olawale Ismail, and Prof. Alain Tschudin all freely shared knowledge during our several brainstorming sessions. I also appreciate the flexibility of Mr. Kavazeua Katjomuise and his colleagues at the UN Office of the Special Adviser on Africa (OSAA). The validation meeting held by the ECA and the special OSAA webinars as well as the several students through the African Institute for Economic

i

Development and Planning (IDEP) training platform all of which further sharpened my thoughts towards putting this volume together.

My original efforts on putting pen to paper to suggest that situational foundation is crucial for analysis as well as accounting for low levels of human development in Nigeria, nay Africa, was equally buoyed by my Special Assistant/Adviser, Mr. Abraham Ameh. He was of immense support in bouncing off ideas as I prepared a PowerPoint presentation for the UNESCO office in Nigeria at which the idea was first presented. He was always ready to support and assist beyond the call of duty.

Dr. Ernest Chinedu, my Consultant on the survey instrument, played a major role. He was very flexible in operationalizing the situational quadruple nexus (SQN) in a way that elicited reactions from Nigerians. He was also very helpful as we pressured several sources to participate in the survey and in making sense of what we have as a result.

Several collaborators made extraordinarily helpful comments on this work. These comments went a long way in improving the overall quality of the study. They include Prof. Raphael O. Olaniyan; JOS; Mr. Adetokunbo Koya; Retired Justice Solomon Abidoye Olugbemi; Dr. Nicholas Erameh; Ambassador Ejeviome Eloho Otobo; Prof. Kayode Oguntuashe, Dr. Christopher Agoha, Mr. Ademisiku Shyllon, Mr. Daniel Akpojiyovwi, Mr. Kola Banjo, and Dr. Anthony Chudi Nweke.

I appreciate and express my gratitude to Jumoke, my tolerant wife, and the larger family, including Dr. Issa Sanogo, Mrs. Adeyinka Sanogo, Mr. Adebola Badejo, and Mrs. Abidemi Ayodele, who served as guinea-pigs for different aspects of this book and to all for accepting my "present but technically absent situation".

Preface

Nigeria is currently riveted by a complexity of problems. Of particular importance among these are variegated conflicts that have made peace and security very elusive in the country. In almost all the six zones making up the country, bloods of Nigerians were flowing from the violent acts of terrorists, bandits, ethnic militia as well as heightened criminal actions of kidnappers and others. There remain palpable tensions as nationalities that make up the Nigerian nation-state are articulating the need to restructure relationships in the country, including some articulating the need to break up the nation-state.

Nigeria has been a failure with respect to efforts to realise development, respect for human rights, as well as resilience in the handling of humanitarian problems. It is now common knowledge that peace/ security and development are interconnected. But so are also the interlinkages between human rights and humanitarianism as well as with peace/security and development. These four pillars account for most of the freedoms that are essential for the good life. How do informed Nigerians see this interconnectedness?

As a Consultant for the ECA from August 2020 through to March 2021, I had the opportunity of building on the idea of a quadruple nexus approach as most useful in understanding the interconnectedness of pillars for the advancement of Africa, hence the need for better coordination. This effort was based on an analysis of West and Central Africa.

Relying on extensive desktop literature review, interviews with focused groups and among practitioners, as well as the use of questionnaires, this study extracted responses from 207 informed Nigerians. Specifically, it interrogated and contextualised the importance of the four-pillar interlinkages. More importantly, however, it explores the situational arrangements within which the quadruple nexus or situational four-pillar interlinkages operate. Aside from the qualitative analysis, the study brings into sharp focus the views of informed Nigerians on the current conflicts enveloping Nigeria.

In addition, the study is highly illuminating and offers refreshing dimensions to existing knowledge towards understanding the crises in Nigeria. It is also hoped that the insights would be helpful towards answers to the problems being faced by Nigeria.

Babafemi A. BADEJO, Ph.D., LL.B.

Chapter One

Introduction

Situational Quadruple Nexus: Towards Understanding Conflicts in Nigeria

Conflicts have been very costly for Nigeria. In the Northeast zone of the country where Boko Haram holds sway, the UN Development Programme (UNDP), estimated that Boko Haram insurgency, over about eleven years ending in December 2020, has claimed about 350,000 deaths with ten percent (35,000), being direct and the remainder being indirect deaths.[1] Some analysts in updating the figures on casualties actually suggest a higher figure. The Civil Society Legislative Advocacy Centre (CISLAC), states that:

> *Civilian lives lost to various armed conflicts in the past decade are over 500,000 ... Over three million people are displaced due to armed conflicts, while over 10 million people depend entirely on humanitarian aid to survive.*[2]

---

1 https://www.premiumtimesng.com/news/headlines/470476-insurgency-has-killed-almost-350000-in-north-east-undp.html. Accessed on January 6, 2022.
2 Salaudeen Hashim, Programme Manager, Defence and Security, CISLAC, New Telegraph, January 5, 2022.

1

Relief Web goes further to suggest a heavy toll on children in the Northeast of Nigeria, as well as capturing more of the ramifications of the Nigerian conflict's profile. It states:

> *In Nigeria's volatile northeast region, children remain direct and indirect targets of unrelenting jihadist fighters. From being killed or kidnapped to forced displacement, where they face complex humanitarian challenges. While many are predisposed to joining armed groups due to socio-economic challenges, others are recruited through coercive measures such as abductions and other life-threatening circumstances. About 300,000 children have been killed and over one million displaced in northeast Nigeria, according to United Nations Children's Emergency Fund (UNICEF). As the jihadist war, bandits' violence, cultism, group conflict, and violent secession struggles and clampdowns rage on, the harsh realities of Nigerian children caught in the web of violent conflicts continue.*

Violent conflict exacerbates the challenges facing children beyond the northeast. There are about 13.2 million out-of-school children in Nigeria, according to Nigeria's Minister of State for Education, Mr. Chukwuemeka Nwajuba. Also, the recent sit-at-home orders in the southeast, attacks, and large-scale kidnapping in schools by bandits are threatening the efforts of many Nigerian children to access education. Since December 2020, about 800 children have been kidnapped in Nigeria. Cumulatively, over ₦1 billion have been demanded as ransom within this period. For example, in February 2021, bandits demanded ₦800 million to release the abducted Kagara schoolboys. Limited access to education prevents children from gaining knowledge and skills for self-reliance, which makes them vulnerable to conflict, its triggers, and consequences.[3]

Many qualitative efforts are being undertaken towards understanding

---

3 https://reliefweb.int/report/nigeria/web-conflicts

the conflictual situation within which Nigeria has found itself.[4] The prescription has tended to focus on the raging conflict almost in isolation, hence the emphasis on physical restructuring of the polity.[5] At times, the absence of peace and security are considered alongside developmental deprivations, including but not limited to having over 13 million children of school age out of school. The interconnectedness of the conflict in Nigeria, (representing the failure on the peace and security pillar), with the other three pillars of development, human rights and the building of humanitarian resilience are hardly deeply considered.

This study addresses the lacunae and more. It recognises that the four pillars are not self-implementing. For this reason, it offers four situational overarching issues that must be considered along the four-pillar interlinkages. Beyond this theoretical descriptive dimension is the soliciting of the views of 207 informed Nigerians on the usefulness of the quadruple nexus within quadruple issues that constitute a situational foundation.

The survey research at the centre of this study was an extract from an originally designed effort to elicit the views of Nigerians, (as part of West and Central Africa), on the interlinkages among development, peace/security, human rights, and humanitarian pillars. The outcome of the survey reinforces the theoretical analysis in this study. It should promote collaborative, complementary, and coherent approaches in the implementation of interventions addressing peace and security, human rights, humanitarian, and development challenges in Nigeria through listening to insights from the people. Responding to the evolving nature of challenges in Nigeria, the survey outcome would also factor in the effects of the COVID-19 pandemic, gender, and youth questions that are prevalent in Nigeria.

The survey outcome strongly supports a quadruple nexus model to

---

4 See, Babafemi A. Badejo, *Rethinking Security Initiatives in Nigeria,* (Lagos: Yintab Books, 2020).
5 See, ibid.

adequately capture and create synergy in reactions on the four pillars in Nigeria. Most fundamental is the endorsement of a quadruple situational foundation for the consideration of the quadruple nexus or pillars. The term nexus is now a popular word used by experts,[6] in referring to the inter-linkages of pillars[7]: development, peace and security, human rights, and humanitarian pillars. The increased pressures on limited global resources due to escalating levels of conflict and crises, in line with the search for integrative, holistic, and sustainable approaches for managing and responding to crises and the aftermaths brought to prominence the triple nexus or interlinkages[8].

This survey result should be of significant use to planners aiming to address conflicts in Nigeria. The report should also provide useful background to local and international aid deliverers. Furthermore, scholars will also have the opportunity of analyzing based on scientifically deduced popular views as opposed to *a priori* deduced theories.

The quadruple nexus, which principally is the addition of human rights to the existing Humanitarian, Development, and Peace (HDP) Nexus, offers a coordinated/interrelated set of practical steps or actions aimed

---

6 The term is used to describe the coming together of humanitarian, development, and peace/security programs, or human rights, development, and peace/security programs.

7 Documents and frameworks have established the relevance of the nexus. The World Humanitarian Summit 2016, Issue Paper May 2016. Also, High-Level Panel on Humanitarian Financing Report to the Secretary-General: Too important to fail - addressing the humanitarian financing gap. January 2016. See also, Guterres, A., (2016), Secretary-General-designate António Guterres' remarks to the General Assembly on taking the oath of office Secretary-General, United Nations, Available at: https://www.un.org/sg/en/content/sg/speeches/2016-12-12/secretary-generaldesignate-antónio-guterres-oath-office-speech [Accessed September 12, 2020] and, The New Way of Working (NWoW) as outlined in the Secretary-General's Report of the WHS Available at https://www.agendaforhumanity.org/sites/default/files/A-71-353%20-%20SG%20Report%20on%20the%20Outcome%20of%20the%20WHS.pdf

8 Cyril Obi, Study on Strengthening and Mainstreaming the Peace, Development and Humanitarian Nexus into Policies and Strategies in Africa, P.3

at reducing people's vulnerability resulting from conflicts, disasters, and poverty. Seeking to achieve these goals requires not only greater collaboration, and engagement between various actors, but also the role of governance, institutions, resources, and external dynamics, with the ultimate goal of realizing human freedom.

The Situational Quadruple Nexus (SQN) approach introduced by Badejo (2020), strengthens collaboration, coherence, and complementarity among the four pillars of development; peace, and security; human rights as well as humanitarianism. In general, the SQN seeks to improve actions for national, sub-regional, regional, and international delivery of assistance.[9] Here, it is being proposed at the national level for Nigeria.

The SQN also maximizes the advantages of each pillar in order to reduce overall vulnerabilities and the number of unmet needs. Applied to Nigeria, the quadruple nexus helps in the analysis and understanding of the root causes of conflicts, development deficit, trampling of human rights, and deficit in resilience towards handling humanitarian affairs, with a view to proffering effective and sustainable solutions.[10] The quadruple nexus must, however, be situated within the quadruple four foundational bedrocks of actions within political systems, especially African ones, in general, and Nigeria, in particular, for this study.

SQN is an explanatory framework for the understanding of how peace and security, development, human rights as well as resilience in humanitarian capacities are interlinked for a synergistic and coherent consideration towards amelioration efforts. However, it is crucial that amelioration efforts must, in turn, be situated within a situational quadruple foundation of governance, (in particular, leadership deficit and corruption); external dynamics that must have a focus on forces

---

9https://www.uneca.org/sites/default/files/uploaded-documents/Subregional-studies/ECA%20Four-Pillar%20Interlinkages%20first%20draft20201215.pdf
10 Babafemi, Badejo (September 21, 2020). "Peace & Security Operate Within a Quadruple Nexus". Presentation at the International Peace Day Town Hall & Community Gathering, Yintab Strategy Consults. Retrieved September 21, 2021.

beyond the borders that accelerate and/or hamper the realisation of the expectations from seeking to improve on the quadruple interlinkages; resources in its many ramifications, including human and capital as well as the existence of institutions that are crucial for the aggregation, articulation, and realisation of interests towards the achievement of freedoms.

Democracy and Utmost Freedom

A major expected outcome of the 2030 Agenda for Sustainable Development, the plan of action for people, the planet, and prosperity, is to strengthen universal peace in larger freedom - a term first popularized by Kofi Annan.[11] The comprehensive nature of the SDGs in pointing to many freedoms beyond those articulated by Kofi Annan has attracted the usage of utmost freedom for our purposes. In this sense, utmost is qualitatively higher than "Larger", that Annan had used. It is positive that Nigeria has keyed into the SDGs. As a result, it is possible to examine the state of utmost freedom in Nigeria.

This study conceptualises the state of utmost freedom as an idyllic state. It is a perfect state. It could be approximated as the summation of all essential freedoms needed for the good life with most of these being pulled together under the SDGs. Utmost freedom is an ideal state on the realisation of freedoms in which all freedoms associated with development, peace and security, human rights, and humanitarianism are optimized. Such an ideal state can be aimed at on earth even if it cannot be realised. An approximation can be documented.

A democracy, for our purposes, is a polity organised to foster a drive towards utmost freedom. For Josiah Ober, the term originally meant the capacity (Kratos) of a people (demos) to accomplish things.[12] For

---

11 United Nations, *Transforming Our World: The 2030 Agenda for Sustainable Development*. A/RES/70/1
12 Veronica Marian, Democracy is often misunderstood, with tragic results, says

Nigeria and most African states, the adoption of liberal democracy was a product of ideological and skillful forcing of a concept down African throats that followed the post-Cold War ideological hunt for neo-colonial dominions. On offer were the enticements of pro-democracy slush funds from western governments and their actors.[13]

Using surveys to explore the views of Africans on democracy with respect to its desirability, governance, quality of life, etc. Afrobarometer[14] discovered resilient aspirations towards democracy in Africa despite declining trends in the quality and status of democracy in Africa. When Africans say they are more committed to democracy, do they say so only because democracy is at the face value, a better option to authoritarian options, or do they mean so, because of the numerous dividends and opportunities inherent in democracy?

On this basis, we may then ask further how satisfied are the people (governed) with democracy beyond the fact that every four or five years, there is an opportunity to gather to select new political leaders in a do or die highly desperate system often shrouded in much corruption, controversies and often time triggers of conflict that results in the loss of many lives? Do the people still firmly believe in the workability of democracy as the ticket to freedoms, good life, accountability, transparency, human security, sustainable development, protection of lives and livelihoods etc? Or are the people beginning to see democracy as a grand deception? Is this new awakening giving room for military political elites to resume coups and counter coups in Africa? Do Africans actually care if it was a khaki wearing military dictator or an agbada or coat wearing civilian that leads provided the job is done? Do Africans have any special attachment to the ideas of democracy?

Stanford classicist. Stanford Report, October 23, 2014.

13 Moses Ochonu, Liberal Democracy has failed in Nigeria. Africa is a Country. 02.07.2020

14 https://afrobarometer.org/blogs/do-africans-want-democracy-and-do-they-think-theyre-getting-it

It is in this frame of mind that Moses Ochonu submitted that several years later, civilian rule in Nigeria has not brought the vaunted benefits of democracy in the form of development, accountability, and freedoms.[15] Ochonu, observes the dangerous legitimising rhetoric of post-Cold War democratisation in such a way that even if democracy fails to improve the lives and civic freedoms of Nigerians and other Africans, there is a consolation prize: the electoral mechanism of voting out non-performing governments, which would overtime entrench a culture of accountability.[16] Herein, lies the fundamental deception that has held the Nigerian state down since 1999. The nature of elections in Nigeria ultimately resulting in the suppression of the will of the people defeats this dangerous rhetoric. Liberal democracy as practised in Nigeria, cannot continue to be paraded as sacrosanct or infallible. It has contributed so much to Nigeria's dysfunctional governance.[17]

The conception of democracy herein, is superior to the current fixations on democracy as periodic elections irrespective of performance failures on accountabilities on many other freedoms that are crucial for the good life. The performance of elected office-holders on all crucial freedoms is very important. Whether elected leaders fail on other important freedoms beyond the freedom to vote should be of concern. Democracy could be a preferred structural arrangement for striving towards utmost freedom.

A state of utmost freedom is unquantifiable. However, values can be attached to the goals enunciated in the SDGs. Such indices, when calculated, can give a composite figure that could allow time comparison as well as inter-state comparative analysis on efforts towards utmost freedom. It is important, however, to note that the indices aimed at approximating utmost freedom can be summed up in a particular epoch. Knowledge and human capacities could, in a future epoch, dictate modifications and/or improvements depending on the subsisting

---

15 Ochonu, *op. cit.*
16 Ibid.
17 Ibid.

knowledge about requisite freedoms.

This study adopts the situational quadruple nexus read along with the Sustainable Development Goals (SDGs) as its analytical framework to lay bare the interlocking relationships of the four pillars: development, peace and security, human rights, and humanitarianism all situated within foundationally important quadruple situations of governance, external dynamics, institutions, and resources as overarching issues. Promoting the SDGs, would be of importance in the situational quadruple nexus and SDGs analysis as illustrated below.

SQN is more than an analytic framework. It is also a model for development. In this respect, it pools together essential pillars of focus to create an all-rounded development of society. It is a model for the achievement of the SDGs in a coherent, effective and synergistic manner. In short, SQN represents when all the four pillars are in focus and the four situational foundations are addressed. The result is an efficient human developmental experience.

Pillars not Self-Implementing

The pillars on which coordination and collaboration are necessary to achieve the SDGs are four: peace/security; development; human rights and humanitarianism. However, the pillars are not sufficient on their own and this is because experiences have shown that not all countries where efforts are deployed on these pillars are able to transform them towards achieving the SDGs. Hence, the need to factor in the conditions necessary to have coherent positive responses or results. In this regard, effective governance, good leadership are crucial to improving the well-being of citizens. Recruiting good leaders remains compelling because good leaders are expected to show total disdain for corruption. Good leadership that eschews corruption and really fights against corruption, (unlike the current Nigerian government that merely pays lip service on countering this vice),[18] will help a nation towards achieving the collaborative coherence of the inter-linkages in the pursuit of the achievement of the SDGs.

Even though the importance of good governance has continually received attention among Nigerian citizens, it should be done holistically, considering both the local and international dimensions. International civil servants assisting in aid delivery must be trained to stop being shy of pointing out adverse facts about governments in power in Nigeria.

However, good governance is not enough. There is the need to pay close attention to the totality of the "situational foundation" on which the pillars rest in Nigeria. In this context, the external dynamics in which the Nigerian state operates is very critical. There is the need to ask what are the best practices on external support for a collaborative effort for actualizing the goals of SDGs, and which negative dimensions are actively taking place as part of efforts by external powers to continue to keep Nigeria, nay Africa down for the ease of exploitation?

The Post-second world war institutions (Bretton Woods Institutions), including the World Bank, the International Monetary Fund (IMF), precursors of the World Trade Organisation (WTO), were set up to ensure the leadership of a few countries who remain the main beneficiaries of the order they set up. Interest payments, especially when compounded, and structured devaluations, will continue to drain Nigeria of resources that could have gone towards addressing development.

For illustration purposes, on the eve of General Ibrahim Babangida's coup d'etat of August 27, 1985, the exchange rate of Naira-Dollar was at 0.89[19]. The preceding government of Major-General Muhammadu

---

18 On documentation that the Buhari Government only pays lip service to corruption, see, Babafemi A. Badejo, "The State of Anti-Corruption in Nigeria: 2015-2019", in Chris Jones, Pregala Pillay and Idayat Hassan, (eds.), Fighting Corruption in African Contexts: Our Collective Responsibility, (Newcastle upon Tyne: Cambridge Scholars Publishing, 2020), Chapter 2.
19 Mike I. Obadan, Overview of Exchange Rate Management in Nigeria from 1986

Buhari was resisting the IMF pressures for parity. General Babangida succumbed to the pressures from the IMF and Western governments by smuggling in the dictates while pretending to be pursuing a home grown Second-Tier Foreign Exchange Market (SFEM).[20] As of January 4, 2022, the official exchange rate as put out by the Central Bank of Nigeria (CBN), was 423.17 naira to purchase one US dollar,[21] and the unofficial rate of exchange was even worse at $1 = N565.

Financial flows are not only in terms of stolen funds but even rules of the games that appear legitimate but actually have been set and foisted by stronger powers who determine how the international financial system operates. It is not that the human mind cannot think through alternatives: the problem is the dominant power relations that follow interests.

Nigerian, nay African leaders see their personal interests as identical to those of the strong countries of the world bent on having Nigeria/Africa, (in spite of resources), at the bottom of global affairs. Having stolen so much money kept in secret safe havens and with such secrets in the hands of the intelligence networks of powerful countries, they cannot be expected to stand up for Nigeria/Africa.

Good governance is not enough to sustain political institutions, and this explains the need to continue to crave for credible political institutions. Undoubtedly, experiences across the globe have shown that strong political institutions help in recruiting and shaping leadership.

Resources are equally important. Good governance can bring some progress, but success is easier if the human and material resources are available for the necessary leadership efforts to have a coherent and coordinated quadruple nexus response.

---

to date. Vol.30, No.3 July-Sept 2006.

20 See, Babafemi A. Badejo, "The Socio-Political Implications of Structural Adjustment Programme (SAP)", *The Journal of Business and Social Studies,* New Series, Vol. 7 No. 1, December 1984 (Published 1990), pp. 57-64.

21 Exchange Rate Archives–Central Bank of Nigeria.

It is abundantly clear that the push on quadruple nexus will not succeed without factoring in and ameliorating on the quadruple situational foundation on which the quadruple nexus rests.

Methodology

The methodological approach for this study is both qualitative and quantitative. Aside from being an informed participant-observer on Nigeria over several years, there have been many interactions with scholars, including the four other Independent Consultants on the quadruple nexus at UNECA and UN OSAA. The theoretical formulation herein has benefited tremendously from these interactions.

For the survey, this study used the instrument designed for the analysis on West and Central Africa. We merely extracted the responses of 207 Nigerian respondents who were part of the larger survey for closer analysis. We adopted a cross-sectional research design that is descriptive in nature.

Designing and drafting of instruments of data collection

The quantitative data came out of the questionnaire originally designed for the ECA report on four-pillar interlinkages in West and Central Africa. The views of Nigerians who participated in the survey were extracted.

The structure of the original survey was as follows:

A. **Questionnaire:** The questionnaire comprised six (6) sessions:

1. <u>Demographics:</u> age, gender, level of educational attainment, income level, occupation, country, state.

2. <u>Peace and security:</u> In this section, the study participants were asked how they perceive peace and security in their country (Nigeria), they were required to rate the level of peace and security

on a scale that was drafted by the statistician. Participants were also asked to outline the particular threats to peace, security, and development in Nigeria and whether these threats were being addressed. Forms of violent crimes and insecurity peculiar to Nigeria were ascertained. Factors underlying threats to peace and insecurity were also examined. Effects of lack of peace and security on human rights, development, and humanitarian affairs were ascertained from this section. Peculiar and particular threats to participants' livelihoods and survivals were also sought.

3. Human rights: In this section, participants were asked questions relating to human rights in Nigeria and if they think that their rights are being abused. They were asked whether there are legal frameworks in Nigeria protecting human rights abuses and how effective the legal framework(s) are in protecting people against human right abuses. Effects of human rights on peace and security, humanitarian and development, in general, were also sought in this section, etc.

4. Humanitarian: This section focused on humanitarians in Nigeria. Participants were requested to outline various humanitarian efforts available in Nigeria, types of humanitarian support deliverers, whether they are local or international, and donor agencies. Correlation between humanitarian gestures and development, do they perceive any hidden agenda from funders and donors? Effects of lack of humanitarians in Nigeria. How humanitarian support can be effectively utilised for the growth and development of Nigeria.

5. Development: In this section, participants were asked to outline factors hindering the development of Nigeria. What is the role of violent crimes and insecurity on the development of Nigeria? How have human rights abuses stalled and hindered development in Nigeria?

6. <u>Interlink between the quadruple nexus:</u> This last section focused on the interlinkages between peace and security, human rights, humanitarian and development pillars with respect to their country which is Nigeria.

Chapter Two

Situational Quadruple Nexus: Some Clarifications

Background/Justification

The triple nexus came as an aftermath of the 2016 Humanitarian summit. The twin resolutions on sustaining peace adopted by the General Assembly 70/262 and Security Council 2282 in April 2016, both articulated the imperatives of coherence and complementarity between the UN's peace and security efforts and its development, human rights, and humanitarian work[1]. These resolutions were pivotal in the push towards synergistic and coherent efforts on analysis as well as operational efforts.

This survey outcome represents the popular reactions in Nigeria to the situational quadruple nexus approach on the basis of coordinated and coherent efforts towards understanding and/or handling of conflicts in the country as well as on the possibilities of achieving the SDGs of Agenda 2030.

---

1 UNECA, Draft Report, virtual Inception Meeting on Subregional Studies on the Interlinkages between the Development, Peace and Security, Human Rights and Humanitarian Pillars. 27 October, 2020

Theory and the Concept of Nexus

The term "Nexus" derives from the Latin word "Nectere" which is to bind, tie or link together. The nexus has gone through much evolution. It started with trying to build synergy between the humanitarian and developmental efforts, especially in a post-conflict situation. The evolutionary situation subsequently included a recognition of the importance of peace for the amelioration of humanitarian problems and the realisation of development. In this situation, the triple nexus brings together its three-pronged approach of—Peace, development, and humanitarian action. The approach seeks to capitalise on the comparative advantages of each pillar – to the extent of their relevance in the specific context – in order to reduce overall vulnerability and the number of unmet needs, strengthen risk management capacities and address root causes of conflict."[2]

The triple nexus, as most commonly used in line with the UN New Ways of Working (NWoW) refers to the interlinkages between humanitarian, development and peace actors. Following the recommendations from the 2016 World Humanitarian Summits (WHS) and in line with the Sustainable Development Goals, 2030 and the AU Agenda 2063 on the Africa We Want, there is the need to focus on leveraging on the joint advantages of the pillars, by effectively eliminating barriers to collaboration.

The central emphasis of the WHS include: placing people at the centre of development and humanitarian actions; providing education – and hope – for children in crises; a grand bargain to improve work efficiency; leaving no one behind; an inclusive "everyone at the table approach"; working together better; going local; the private sector as a meaningful partner; innovating today for a better tomorrow and finally, reducing

---

2 Organisation for Economic Co-operation and Development (OECD), 2019. DAC recommendation on the humanitarian-development-peace nexus. Available at: https://legalinstruments.oecd.org/en/instruments/OECD-LEGAL-5019

risks and increasing resilience.[3]

Nexus thinking and action represents a paradigm shift for meeting peoples' needs whether in situations of crises or in implementing plans for growth and advancement of societies, subregions, and regions. In conflict situations, in particular, the presence and involvement of development and peace actors in protracted crises would be a positive move for the sustainability of solutions. The Triple Nexus would then allow the space for "burden-sharing" among humanitarian, development, and peace actors, where they can complement and learn from each other.[4]

The nexus concept emphasizes the importance of understanding connections, synergies, and trade-offs. If well implemented, it could reduce negative surprises and promote integrated or collaborative planning, management, and governance in the delivery of the SDGs.[5] The nexus approach helps in uncovering synergies and co-benefits, as well as detecting and minimizing harmful trade-offs[6]. supporting in identifying unexpected consequences[7], bringing together actors involved in different sectors, nexus approaches can promote collaboration, cooperation, coordination and policy coherence for effective governance

---

3 Alain Tschudin, presentation to the United Nations Office of the Special Adviser on Africa (OSAA), Strengthening the capacity of African countries to design and implement policies that promote the nexus between peace, humanitarian work, development, and human rights for accelerated implementation of the SDGs. 15th March 2021.
4 International Council of Voluntary Agencies, Learning Livestream. Cited in DCA Actalliance. The Triple Nexus, Localisation, and Local Faith Actors: The intersections between faith, humanitarian response, development, and peace. A review of the literature
5 Jianguo Liu, Vanessa Hull, et al, Nexus approaches to global sustainable development. Nature Sustainability | VOL 1 | SEPTEMBER 2018 | p.466 | www.nature.com/natsustain
6 Daher, B. T. & Mohtar, R. H. Water-energy-food (WEF) nexus tool 2.0: guiding integrative resource planning and decision-making. Water Int. 40, 748–771 (2015)
7 Rasul, G. Food, water, and energy security in South Asia: a nexus perspective from the Hindu Kush Himalayan region. Env. Sci. Pol. 39, 35–48 (2014).

and management[8]

However, it is important to note that the nexus thinking is not an out of the blues approach. It is only a more refined approach to achieving progress on the pillars. In fact, it has been proposed severally under different appellations—Linking relief, rehabilitation, and development, humanitarian-development nexus, etc. Some actors have considered adding other elements in the nexus (like migration, human rights, security, stabilisation, etc.)[9]. But in this study, we are focusing on the nexus approach that progressed from the UN articulated triple HDP Nexus into a Quadruple Nexus of Humanitarian, Development, Peace, and Human rights.

However, it is important to note that the concept of quadruple nexus is in itself a culmination of progress and transformation in the collaborative usage of the pillars. In this regard Boutros Boutros-Ghali's (1992)[10] was seminal. He articulated the link between Peace and Development. For Boutrous Boutrous-Ghali, his approach towards preventive diplomacy, peacemaking, and peacekeeping, was targeted at supporting actions and structures which will strengthen and consolidate peace in such a way as to prevent possible relapse of conflicts. In order words, address the deepest causes of conflicts.[11]

"Peacebuilding is a process that facilitates the establishment of durable peace and tries to prevent the recurrence of violence by addressing root causes and effects of conflicts through reconciliation, institutions building, and political as well as economic transformation" (An Agenda

---

8 Ringler, C., Bhaduri, A. & Lawford, R. The nexus across water, energy, land, and food (WELF): potential for improved resource use efficiency? Curr. Opin. Env. Sustain. 5, 617–624 (2013). See also Ross, A. & Connell, D, The evolution and performance of river basin management in the Murray-Darling Basin. Ecol. Soc. 21, 39 (2016).

9 ICVA Humanitarian Learning, Learning Stream: Navigating the Nexus Topic 1: The "nexus" explained.

10 Boutros Boutros-Ghali, *An Agenda for Peace,*

11 The conceptual origins of peacebuilding. www.peacebuilidnginitiative.org

for Peace, 1992)

Subsequently, the UNDP Report on Human Security, (1994), showed the greater interactions between issues of traditional security and issues related to development, human rights, freedom, and democracy. The 1994 report recognised the importance of human security as an approach. It stated that security is about people and less of territory, security is more of development and less of arms. This thinking brought a new paradigm of sustainable human development, with peace dividends.[12] Human security also involves Freedom from Fear and Want in a number of aspects of human daily lives and living. In this respect, Freedom from Fear of Hunger, Poverty, Diseases like Covid-19 and other viruses like Ebola, environmental degradation and accompanying crimes, terrorism coupled with the State on violations of human rights, resilience in managing all forms of natural and man-made disasters, etc. This came off the back of the 1994 HDR and the 2003 report of the Commission on Human Security "Human Security Now" which argued that the threat agenda should be expanded to cover hunger, diseases, and natural disasters, which kill far more people than wars, genocide, and terrorism combined. Today, this position is subject to debate, given the increasing threats of terrorism. However, what is important, is that the two approaches to the understanding of security, be treated complementary based on specificities.

"For countries emerging from conflicts, peacebuilding offers the chance to establish new institutions, social, political and judicial, that can give impetus to development... Pulling up the roots of conflicts goes beyond immediate post-conflict requirements and the repair of war-torn societies. The underlying conditions that led to conflicts must be addressed. As the causes of conflicts are varied, so must be the means of addressing them. (An Agenda for Development, 1994)

Building on the need for synergistic thinking on the post-conflict situation,

---

12 UNDP. 1994. Human Development Report 1994: New Dimensions of Human Security. http://www.hdr.undp.org/en/content/human-development-report-1994

the report of the Panel on United Nations Peace Operations (Brahimi Report) refined the definition of peacebuilding as "Activities undertaken on the far side of the conflict to reassemble the foundations of peace and provide the tools for building on those foundations something that is more than just the absence of war"[13]

Kofi Annan in his 2003 Review of Technical Cooperation in the United Nations, called for an action plan to identify the ways in which different parts of the UN system might work together to devise country-specific peacebuilding strategies". Connecting to 2004, after the Report of the High-Level Panel on Threats, Challenges and Change was released, Kofi Annan produced his report "In Larger Freedom" in May 2005 articulating the link between Peace, Development and Human Rights. The Heads of States at the World Summit endorsed this in September 2005.

The 2007 report of the Peacebuilding Commission, holds that "The Peacebuilding Commission will marshal resources at the disposal of the international community to advise and propose integrated strategies for post-conflict recovery, focusing attention on construction, institution building and sustainable development, in countries emerging from conflicts" The Commission will bring together the UN's broad capacities and experiences in conflict prevention, mediation, peacekeeping, human rights, rule of law, humanitarian assistance, reconstruction and long-term development"[14]

On January 18, 2008, the UN Secretary-General said "the Peacebuilding Commission embodies all aspects of the UN's work: peace, development and human rights. By integrating them into one coherent approach you are helping to close gaps in the international response to countries emerging from conflicts"[15]

Armatya Sen also added to the thinking on development as freedom. Sen

---

13 The conceptual origins of peacebuilding. www.peacebuilidnginitiative.org
14 The conceptual origins of peacebuilding. www.peacebuilidnginitiative.org
15 The conceptual origins of peacebuilding. www.peacebuilidnginitiative.org

in the introduction of his book on Economic Inequality puts it thus: "the relationship between inequality and rebellion is indeed a close one"[16] Sen's humanistic approach calls to book the numerous "unfreedoms"—hunger, tyranny, exploitations pushed by present-day liberal, capitalist economic-development approaches. A recent report by a group of UN-appointed independent rights experts titled, "Rush for new profits posing threat to human rights, UN expert warns", argues that the finance industry's demand for new sources of capital worldwide to satisfy investors, is having a serious negative impact on the enjoyment of human rights. For example, the right to safe drinking water and sanitation, food, adequate housing, development, and a healthy and sustainable environment, etc. There is the exploitation of the marginalised, unfair effect on housing, food crisis, and the commodification of nature[17]

The UN Humanitarian Development and Peace (HDP) nexus which gained more patronage and application under the UN and World Bank New Way of Working (NWoW), focuses on addressing peoples' vulnerability before, during, and after crises. The HDP relates to structural shifts across the aid systems, changing how aid is planned and financed.

The 2016 World Humanitarian Summit is the most recent commitment to a more coherent approach to meeting immediate needs simultaneously, ensuring longer-term investment addressing the systemic causes of conflict and vulnerability—poverty, inequality and poor accountability. The WHS emphasized the prevention and end of conflict, respect for rules of war, leaving no one behind, from aid to ending needs and investing in humanity.

The dual resolutions passed by the General Assembly and the Security Council in April 2016, (Resolutions 70/262 and 2282) recognised the imperatives of coherence and complementarity between the UN's peace

---

16 Amartya Sen, Economic Inequality, 1973, p.1
17 UN News, Rush for new profits posing threat to human rights, UN experts warn. 20 October 2021.

and security efforts and its development, human rights, and humanitarian work[18].

The importance of the human rights pillar has been noted from the inception of the United Nations. Kofi Annan, as Secretary-General, gave a fillip to human rights with respect to peace and development thus leading to its import as one of the four interlinked pillars. The UNECA's push for the implementation of a four-pillar approach adds humanitarianism and leads to a critical boost in addressing conflicts in Africa.

The quadruple nexus or the four-pillar interlinkages approach is not only important for analysis by showing the interconnectedness of all the pillars in making sense of the situation in Nigeria or Africa. The quadruple nexus approach also helps with operational efforts. It makes it easy to identify the numbers of unmet needs and possibilities in addressing them in a synergistic and coherent manner. It also strengthens risk management capacities.

The increased pressures on limited global resources due to escalating levels of conflict and crises, in concert with the search for integrative, holistic, and sustainable approaches for managing and responding to crises and the aftermaths made more relevant, the application of the triple nexus[19].

The quadruple nexus approach, as Badejo argues, represents a needed growth on the triple nexus approach.[20] We adopt a quadruple nexus

---

18 UNECA, Draft Report, virtual Inception Meeting on Subregional Studies on the Interlinkages between the Development, Peace and Security, Human Rights and Humanitarian Pillars. 27 October 2020

19 Cyril Obi, Study on Strengthening and Mainstreaming the Peace, Development and Humanitarian Nexus into Policies and Strategies in Africa, p. 3. He used nexus though we are using pillar interlinkages in this study.

20 Babafemi Adesina BADEJO, "A study report on The Interlinkages between the Development, Peace and Security, Human Rights and Humanitarian Pillars in the West and Central Africa Subregions" submitted to The United Nations Economic

approach to accommodate the four pillars within the situational foundation issues that are necessary for an optimal operational state.

The four situational foundations are as important as the four pillars. Here, the focus is on the salience of 1) governance, especially the adequacy or inadequacy of leadership, the level of corruption, and other salient issues like respect for rule of law; 2) external dynamics, including positive and negative stimuli from the outside environment within which national/subregional and regional entities are situated; 3) existence or lack of institutions to support societal improvements, and 4) availability or unavailability resources that are necessary for operational needs on the realisation of pillar activities.

Sustainable Development Goals (SDGs)

With projections of an explosion of the world population and pressures on the earth, global challenges such as heightening food insecurity, water scarcity and fossil fuel use, poor access to healthcare, and environmental protection, are becoming more pressing and deeply interlinked.[21] The realities of climate change and its social, political, and economic consequences make the challenges and interlinkages more complex.[22]

The global sustainable development agenda seeks to end poverty, protect the planet, ensure sustainable peace and prosperity by 2030. The 17 goals address issues pertinent to the four pillars of peace and security, development, human rights, and humanitarianism in Africa. Sustainable development will always remain elusive without peace and security, and peace and security will be at risk without sustainable development. The 2030 Agenda for Sustainable Development recognises the need to build peaceful, just, and inclusive societies that provide equal access to justice

---

Commission for Africa, March 2021.
21 Liu, J. et al. Systems integration for global sustainability. Science 347, 1258832 (2015)
22 IPCC Climate Change 2014: Synthesis Report (eds Core Writing Team, Pachauri, R. K. & Meyer L. A.) (IPCC, 2015).

based on respect for human rights (including the right to development), on effective rule of law and good governance at all levels and on transparent, effective and accountable institutions[23] Development is also considered as a conflict prevention mechanism. Through equitable and sustainable development, security is enhanced, directly serving as a conflict prevention instrument.

Scholars such as Van Zanten & Van Tulder (2020) suggest that "the success of the Sustainable Development Goals (SDGs) depends on solving the 'nexus' challenge". They seek to understand "how the positive interactions between SDGs can be optimized, and negative interactions minimized, in order to create co-benefits and reduce trade-offs"[24]

The Development Pillar

Development seeks to provide long-term support to developing countries in proffering sustainable solutions for addressing issues that promote life, in particular, healthy life. In addition, are moves towards the eradication of poverty, supporting livelihoods, and providing basic services, with a particular focus on those in greatest need and furthest behind.[25]. On the other hand, non-development conditions explains situations of self-seeking elite, dependent and consumerist in nature, who cannot mobilise the masses for genuine development.[26]

---

23 Para 35, United Nations, Transforming Our World: The 2030 Agenda for Sustainable Development. A/RES/70/1

24 Alain Tschudin, presentation at United Nations Office of the Special Adviser on Africa (OSAA) webinar, Strengthening the capacity of African countries to design and implement policies that promote the nexus between peace, humanitarian work, development, and human rights for accelerated implementation of the SDGs. 15th March 2021. P.18

25 Organisation for Economic Co-operation and Development (OECD), 2019. DAC recommendation on the humanitarian-development-peace nexus. Available at: https://legalinstruments.oecd.org/en/instruments/OECD-LEGAL-5019 p. 16

26 Agoha, C (2012) "Elite, Leadership, and Governance: The Triple Dilemma of Democratic Development in Nigeria", in Solofo Randranja (ed.), *African Power Elite:*

Classical theories of development consider development within the framework of economic growth and development. According to these theories, development is a synonym for the economic growth that every state in a particular stage has to undergo. These theories consider developing countries as countries limited by poor allocation of resources emerging as a result of the firm hand of government and corruption, inefficient and insufficient economic initiatives, but also political, institutional, and economic austerity, whereby being captured in dependence and domination of developed wealthy states.[27]

Development most commonly is perceived as structural transformation, human development, development of democracy and governance, and development as environmental sustainability.[28]

The understanding of sustainable development continues to evolve, with growing realisation of the complexities of human activities and interactions with the environment. For example, The World Commission on Environment and Development, (WCED, 1987) Report "Our Common Future", sees sustainable development as a development that meets the needs of the present without compromising the ability of future generations to meet their own needs.[29] Sustainable development was later described more as a conceptual socio-economic system which ensures the sustainability of goals in the form of real income achievement and improvement of educational standards, health care, and the overall quality of life[30]

As hinted earlier, development simply means expanding people's choices,

---

Identity, Domination, and Accumulation, CODESRIA, Darkar.
27 Todaro, M.P. & Smith, S.C. (2003). Economic Development (8th ed.). Harlow: Pearson Education Limited.
28 Tomislav Klarin, The Concept of Sustainable Development: From its Beginning to the Contemporary Issues. Zagreb International Review of Economics & Business, Vol. 21, No. 1, pp. 68, 2018
29 Report of the World Commission on Environment and Development "Our Common Future" United Nations, 1987. P.15
30 Pearce, D. (1989). Tourism Development. London: Harlow.

removing various types of limitations, unfreedoms that reduce the opportunities people have to utilise their human capacities, and chances of living the kind of quality lives they want.

International organisations like the World Bank, International Monetary Fund (IMF), World Trade Organisation (WTO) that are at the forefront of development, all have different mandates and may approach the issue of development with different perspectives both operationally and analytically. However, for most of the post-world-war II era and international organisations, development has been defined in terms of a long-term view with a focus on socio-economic structural transformation. This focus also responded to the UN MDGs and now UN SDGs.

Very interestingly, the German Federal Ministry for Economic Cooperation and Development (BMZ) holds that development policy seeks to improve economic, social, ecological and political conditions to help remove the structural causes of conflicts and promote, peaceful, conflict management.

The emphasis of the work of the United Nations Office of the Special Adviser on Africa (OSAA) in the areas of peace, security, and development, is a consolidation of late Kofi Annan's efforts and policy initiatives around peace, development, and human rights as well as demonstrating of the nexus between them[31].

The Peace and Security Pillar

Peace and Security is perhaps the most talked about issue on Africa's search for development. This is because of the elusiveness of sustainable peace and security in Africa. By far one of the most used terms in international discourse. Galtung and other scholars have provided conceptual clarifications on the subject of peace and conflicts. Peace can be positive or negative. Unlike negative peace, which refers

---

31 Ejeviome Eloho Otobo and Oseloka H. Obaze.," Kofi Annan: In Service of the World". Kujenga Amani Social Science Research Council. August 29, 2018.

to the absence of violence, positive peace defines the set of attitudes, institutions, and structures which when strengthened, will lead to a more peaceful society.[32] And this results in cooperation for mutual benefit and a situation where individuals and society are in harmony[33].

Security in the most rounded understanding covers varying critical issues as individual security, collective/group security, national security (response to internal and external threats), social, political, economic, legal, judicial, food, financial, environment, health, and humanitarian affairs.[34] This rounded conception that goes beyond security qua security to human security emphasises rights-based development and humanitarian resilience.

Security is more about people and less of territory, security is more of development and less of arms. This thinking brought a new paradigm of sustainable human development, with a peace dividend.[35] Human security also involves Freedom from Fear and Freedom from Want in a number of aspects of human daily lives and living. In this respect, freedom from fear of hunger, poverty, diseases like Covid-19 and other viruses like Ebola, environmental degradation and accompanying crimes, terrorism coupled with the State on violations of human rights, resilience in managing all forms of natural and man-made disasters, etc.

Kofi Annan, former UN Secretary-General had stated:

There is no development without peace, but there is also no peace without development[36] *The current UN Secretary-General*

---

32 Ibid.

33 J. Galtung, "Twenty-five years of Peace Research: Ten Challenges and some Responses" Journal of Peace Research, 1985.

34 Dr. Zeïni MOULAYE and IGP Mahamadou NIAKATE | Shared Governance of Peace and Security, The Malian Experience.

35 UNDP, *Human Development Report 1994: New Dimensions of Human Security.* http://www.hdr.undp.org/en/content/human-development-report-1994

36 United Nations News, 'Peace is at risk and violated in many places, but we will not give up, says UN chief, Guterres.' https://news.un.org/en/story/2018/09/1020092

added: "Inclusive and sustainable development not only is an end in itself but also happens to be the best defense against the risk of violent conflict [37]

Peacebuilding, according to BMZ, is an attempt to encourage the development of the structural conditions, attitudes, and modes of political behaviour that may permit peaceful, stable, and ultimately prosperous social and economic development. Peacebuilding covers security, socio-economic foundations, political frameworks for long-term peace and reconciliation.

For the World Bank and the IMF, concepts such as post-conflict reconstruction or recovery entail activities that support the transition from conflict to peace in an affected country through the rebuilding of the socio-economic framework of the society, or activities to restore assets and production levels in the disrupted economy.

The Human Rights Pillar

Human rights are what every human being needs to live a dignified and fulfilled life and to participate fully in society. They are entitlements – you have them just because you are human (Amnesty International Speak Free 2011). Human rights are rights that every human being has by virtue of his or her human dignity. Human rights are the most fundamental rights of human beings.

The Universal Declaration of Human Rights (UDHR), 1948, defines human rights as "rights derived from the inherent dignity of the human person." However, the conceptualisation and perception of human rights continue to evolve with the non-stopping process of human development. From a legal understanding, human rights can be defined as the sum of individual and collective rights recognised by

[Accessed September 24, 2020)
37 Peacebuilding and Sustainable Peace, Report of the Secretary-General January 18, 2018

sovereign States and enshrined in their constitutions and in international law. Governments and other duty bearers are under an obligation to respect, protect and fulfill human rights, which form the basis for legal entitlements and remedies in case of non-fulfillment.

However, many have suggested that this cannot be the only way. If human rights exist only because of enactment, their availability is contingent on domestic and international political developments. Many people have looked for a way to support the idea that human rights have roots that are deeper and less subject to human decisions like legal enactments. The best form of existence for human rights would combine robust legal existence with the sort of moral existence that comes from widespread acceptance based on strong moral and practical reasons.[38]

Human rights are inalienable rights entitled to by all human beings, whatever the nationality, place of residence, sex, national or ethnic origin, colour, religion, language, or any other status. As such, human rights are universal, interrelated, interdependent and indivisible and constitute the basis of the concepts of peace, security and development (UNODC). These civil, political, economic, social and cultural rights are all interrelated, interdependent and indivisible. Also relevant in this context, is the United Nations Secretary General's Human Rights Due Diligence Policy (HRDDP) which emphasizes the importance of maintaining the legitimacy, credibility, and public image of the global organisation, and measured through consistency in reporting and promoting human rights.

Africa and the UDHR

Most of Africa was not effectively involved in the design of the UDHR and action for its education and enforcement. In fact, only Egypt and two sub-Saharan countries, Ethiopia and Liberia, voted in favour of the

---

38 See Stanford Encyclopedia of Philosophy, Human Rights. First published Fri Feb 7, 2003, reviewed Thursday, April 11, 2019.

adoption of the UDHR in 1948[39] South Africa stayed away together with the Soviet bloc. All the other countries were still under colonial rule and represented de jure by the colonial powers. However, as more African countries became independent, they joined the UN and enthusiastically became part of most of the major human rights treaties.

The 1981 African Charter on Human and Peoples' Rights

The African Charter on Human and People's Rights (Charter) is the most significant legal framework or tool for the promotion of Human Rights in Africa.

Following the pattern in the rest of the world, the Organisation of African Unity (OAU) adopted the African Charter on Human and People's Rights (ACHPR) on 27 June 1981, marking the dawn of a new era in the field of human rights in Africa. It was adopted on 21 October 1986, and as of 29 April, 2002 had 53 States parties.

The Charter contains a catalogue of rights, cutting across a wide spectrum not only of civil and political rights but also of economic, social, and cultural rights. The African Charter further has the African Commission on Human and Peoples' Rights as its offshoot, "to promote human and peoples' rights and ensure their protection in Africa" (art. 30).

The African Charter on Human rights protection also highlights, Regional Courts and Human Rights protection, Sub-regional organisations, and Human Rights Protection, specifically the ECOWAS Community Court of Justice (ECCJ), and Human Rights

It took five years for a majority of the member states to ratify the Charter, and 13 years for the African Commission to publish its first decision.[40]

---

39 Session of the UN General Assembly, 10 December 1948, Palais de Chaillot, Paris cited in …

40 Nico Horn, Human rights education in Africa, https://www.kas.de/c/document_library/get_file?uuid=a772df28-cfc4-4205-8004-8268ff2bb18b&groupId=252038

Only in 1999, when Eritrea ratified the Charter, did it finally attain the full ratification of all 53 OAU member states. The Charter specifies a number of rights. For example,

- Article 8, very importantly, makes the case for freedom of conscience and religion.
- Article 13 stipulates the right to participation in governance, access to public services. Social and economic rights such as right to own property
- (Art. 14), right to work
- (Art. 15), right to enjoy physical and mental health
- (Art. 16), right to education and cultural life of a community
- (Art. 17) and right to economic, social, and cultural development
- (Art. 22), equality of persons
- (Art. 19), right to life and integrity
- (Art. 4), right to liberty and security of persons
- (Art. 6), right to a fair hearing
- (Art.7), freedom of association and free assembly

The theme of the 2021 International Human Rights Day, "Equality, Reducing Inequalities, Advancing Human Rights" touches on prevailing human rights challenges in Nigeria. At various levels of organisation of the Nigerian society, including levels of governance, are replate of human rights challenges met with such a height of impunity and arbitrariness. The Nigerian state continues to fail in three critical areas which are pivotal in protecting human needs. Human needs together with justice are instrumental in enhancing human rights. The three critical areas include the Human Development Index, Corruption Perception Index, and the Democracy Index. Adding to the issue of needs, Moses Ochonu interestingly with an allusion to Maslow's hierarchy of needs argues that for most Africans their most critical needs are existential.

Such that human rights are worried about as an afterthought to the most pressing needs.

> *All over the world, including the west, the discourse of needs precede the discourse on rights. Because of the obvious developmental challenges of Africa, for the vast majority of Africans, the discourse of individual rights is a discourse of luxury that is a distraction, at the moment, from their most pressing need".* [41]

The Humanitarian Pillar

The core of humanitarianism is to save lives, alleviate sufferings and maintain human dignity during and after man-made crises and disasters, including those caused by natural hazards, as well as to prevent and strengthen preparedness for when such situations occur."[42]

The UNHCR, the UN Refugee Agency has continued to report the climate crisis and displacements as two major humanitarian challenges. Disaster often results in situations of many people fleeing their homes and posing a refugee crisis. Climate change has the potential to intensify conflicts as people compete more for scarce resources. Therefore, Disaster Risk Reduction and Resilience Building must be increasingly explored as antidotes.

Conflicts are rife in Nigeria. They have environmental impacts even before the outbreaks of wars.[43] Environmentally damaging footprints accompany military and armed insurrection preparedness. The damages to the environment linger on after conflicts and rob lives and livelihoods.

---

41 See Anne Kidmose's Interview with Moses Ochonu "The Democratic lie Story", Danish weekly newspaper, Weekendavisen, October 1, 2021

42 Active Learning Network for Accountability and Performance (ALNAP), 2018. Defining humanitarian aid. Available at: www.alnap.org/help-library/defining-humanitarian-aid

43 "How does War Damage the Environment". Available at https//www.ceobs.org/how-does-war-damage-the-environment. Accessed 22/10/2020.

This situation denies development even at its rudimentary levels. Respect for human rights equally suffers. The interconnectedness can also be harnessed for positive outcomes in the lives of people.

Analytical framework: Situational Quadruple Nexus & SDGs

The Quadruple Nexus as shown in the diagram below reflects the interlocking relationship of the four pillars: development, peace and security, human rights, and humanitarian all situated within a foundationally important environment of governance and institutions, resources, and external dynamics, as overarching issues. In our consideration of the nexus, we cannot understate the role of the situational foundations or overarching issues of Governance (leadership, corruption), Resources, Institutions, and External Dynamics.

Success in driving the situational quadruple nexus approach takes us towards the maximisation of the SDGs as shown in the first diagram.

SITUATIONAL QUADRUPLE NEXUS & SDGs

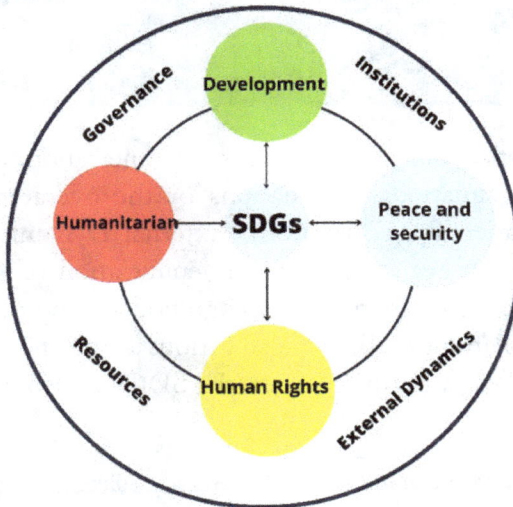

The summation of all the SDGs is equal to the realisation of optimal freedoms that are essential for a good, if not a perfect life on earth. If you like, this state will signify a move towards utmost freedom as shown in the second diagram[44].

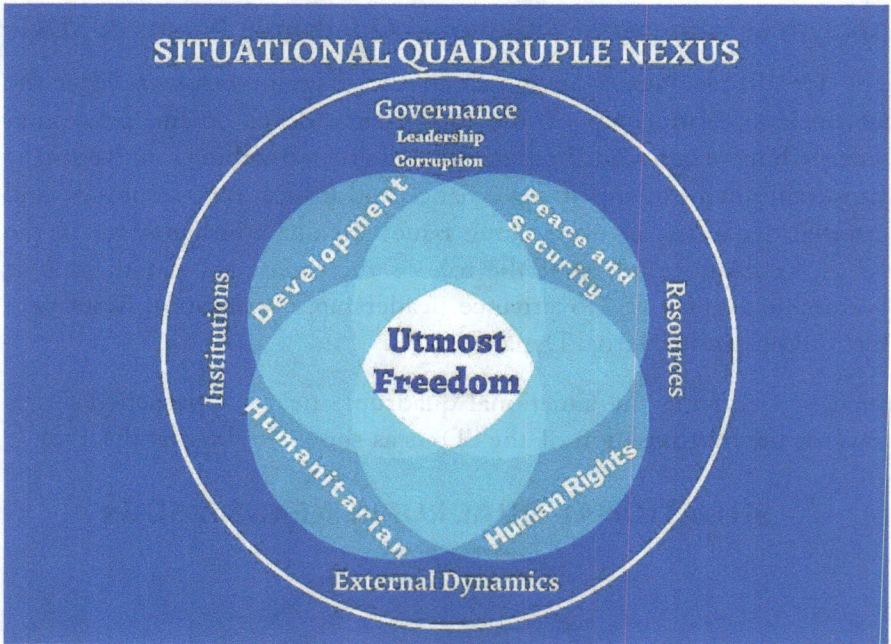

In any consideration of the nexus approach, one cannot overemphasize the role of the situational foundations or the overarching issues of Governance (leadership, corruption); External Dynamics; Institutions and Resources. This reality leads to the enunciation of the Situational Quadruple Nexus. The increasing recognition of the fact that deeper and stronger collaborations amongst various actors towards collective outcomes would enhance progress on the SDGs is also very significant.

44 See, Babafemi A. Badejo in http://yintabstrategyconsults.com/peace-security-operate-within-a-quadruple-nexus/ and https://www.uneca.org/sites/default/files/uploaded-documents/Subregional-studies/Inception%20report%20WestandCentral%20Africa%20Interlinkages%20Study.pdf

And in this regard, there is the clear recognition that pillar coordinated efforts or coherence and synergistic efforts must factor in the specificities of operational situations in specific countries.

Governance: Leadership/Corruption

Visionary leadership is crucial on overall management of purposeful efforts towards utmost freedom. Leadership failure/deficit results in the opposite. Efficient management of gender, generational gaps and ethnicities, with the latter constantly manipulated results in tensions, conflicts and war all of which result in humanitarian problems and arrests of development.

Corruption has been a major threat to progress on the four pillars. Corruption impedes economic, social and environmental developments. Investigation of the impacts of corruption on the multi-dimensional macroeconomic indicators of development has always been a crucial area of research amongst economists and policymakers worldwide[45].

Reinikka and Smith (2004) portrayed a negative relationship between corruption and economic development by asserting that rising corruption rates severely dampen national incomes in economies[46]. Likewise, corruption when reduced could result in a boost of societal development. According to Gupta et al. (2000),[47] Curbing the rates of

---

45 Muntasir Murshed, "Impacts of Corruption on Sustainable Development: A Simultaneous Equations Model Estimation Approach" Available at https://www.researchgate.net/publication/324606339_Impacts_of_Corruption_on_Sustainable_Development_A_Simultaneous_Equations_Model_Estimation_Approach#:~:text=Corruption%20is%20perceived%20to%20be,development%20all%20around%20the%20globe.&text=In%20light%20of%20the%20estimated,Asian%2C%20African%20and%20LAC%20subpanels. Accessed 23/10/2020.
46 'Public Expenditure Tracking Surveys in Education', UNESCO International Institute for Educational Planning, Paris, Cited in Muntasir Murshed, supra, page 3.
47 Gupta, S, Davoodi, H and Tiongson, E 2000, 'Corruption and Provision of Health Care and Education Services', IMF Working Paper No. 116., Cited in Muntasir

corruption within an economy can lead to social development in the form of lower child and infant mortality rates and reduced the percentage of babies with low birth-weights as well as ensure a decreased number of school dropouts.

On the other hand, an increase in corruption in a nation adversely impacts the SDGs of the country. For example, when resources are diverted from development programmes for the selfish benefit of a few, the development aspirations of the people are impacted. It also leads to disenfranchisement, human rights abuses, conflict situations, with grave consequences for peace and security, humanitarianism and fuels the vicious cycle of underdevelopment.

Corruption is not easily understood. This study adopts the definition earlier proffered by Badejo:

> *the abuse of power and/or authority, including manipulation of rules or opportunities, or extortion from another in the public, private or social realms for self or filial/familial relations or inducement (bribery), by another in furtherance of undue gain to the self or a desired third party* [48].

Failure to eschew corruption, lack of transparencies and failure of accountability are the bane of opportunities towards utmost freedom. There is an inverse relationship between corruption and the realisation of rule of law. The more the corruption in a society, the less the operation of rule of law in such a society.

State Governors in Nigeria pocket well over N208.8bn every year as security votes with nothing to show for it, according to Civil Society Legislative Advocacy Centre (CISLAC). Contra the 371,800-strong

---

Murshed, supra.

48 Babafemi A. Badejo, "Persistence of Corruption in Nigeria: Towards a Holistic Focus", in Sunday Bobai Agang et. al., (eds.), A Multidimensional Perspective on Corruption in Africa: Wealth, Power, Religion and Democracy, (Newcastle upon Tyne: Cambridge Scholars Publishing, 2019), p. 141.

Nigerian Police Force with a budget of N409bn for 2020.

But the tragic irony is that half of the 371,000 officers of the Nigerian Police, paid and maintained by the federal budget of N409bn are deployed protecting and serving state governors, local government chairmen and their families, principal officers, top state party men and their families while the Governors pocket N208bn for nothing and the rest of the citizens remain at the mercy of criminals.

This underscores the need to shift ethnoreligious tinted fixations away from the centre and focus as well on the looting of states' resources with impunity by governors, making states' governors accountable. Without electing governors with integrity, the quest for development and better standards of living will continue to be a mirage.

External Dynamics: Impact of External Interests

External dynamics are the totality of influences, whether positive or negative, affecting the policy choices of a state. They are opportunities and challenges that a state has to contend with. In other words, relationships that a state or groups of states have in place with major international interests that could offer positive support or overwhelm a state.

We cannot exhaust the discussion on the four-pillar interlinkages approach as it relates to sustainable development in Africa, without making references to the historical angle of colonisation and its continued impact. Since independence, these countries have maintained tight trade, monetary and diplomatic relations as well as commitment for goodwill socio-economic development with former colonisers, mainly European countries. It is to be noted in addition, that different levels of military relationships ranging from defense pacts, the presence of bases to training between countries and their former coloniser have impacts. There are countries that continue to pay for having been granted independence etc. In effect, available resources for investments, etc., are limited.

However, this is not to undermine the place of national governance. The capacities of governments and institutions do matter and could represent the extent to which the state is able to move people towards utmost freedom.

Other international influence comes from the European Union, The United States, and China. The coordination between states is affected by common challenges. For example, Nigeria and states in the Chad basin, cooperating to tackle the Boko Haram menace, represent some forms of external influence as well.

These relationships must be factored into calculations with respect to strategic and operational plans that seek to make the best out of a quadruple nexus synergistic approach to support delivery. Other salient issues in external dynamics include: foreign policies of states, versus nature of global peace and security, external 'aides' as well as drains in the form of neo-colonialism and brain drain as they affect development. And when development is adversely affected, all other pillars become problematic.

Institutions

The successful national-level implementation of the interlinkages of the four pillars of development, peace and security, human rights, and humanitarianism, depends a lot on the level of commitment of government and institutions. The institutional capacities and how appropriate and functional these institutional arrangements are, are very critical.

Primary functions attributed to institutions are the facilitation of collective action and the reduction of transaction costs. Further, it is suggested that it is not the mere establishment of institutions that matters for development, but the public perceptions about their credibility[49].

---

49 Government at a Glance 2013, Trust in Government, Policy Effectiveness and the Governance Agenda. OECD 2013.

The problem of efficient institutions is not limited to the arms of government like the Executive, Legislature, and the Judiciary. It includes entities/bodies created by the Executive that is corruption-free and ready to deliver on projects for development, security, etc.

Driving partnerships with non-governmental, private, and financial organisations at the national and international levels is very critical for governance and progress on the four pillars.

Social institutions like religious bodies; Civil Society Organisations (CSOs) are also very important. CSOs and NGOs play critical roles as service providers, the watchdogs in governance. The increasing failure of governance, corruption, and numerous threats to peace and development, should lead to increased roles of NGOs and CSOs.

Capacity building for leadership development and efficiency, is one very critical role of institutions. We shall examine these institutions (public institutions, CSOs, religious institutions and the private sectors) and how they can support progress in the work for the interlinkages.

Resources

The combination of both human and material resources is very critical for the interlinkages. Issues affecting material resources, such as developmental funding, higher demand exceeding the scope of investment, poor capacity in governance, and corruption are very consequential. This is an opportunity to understand the critical role resources play across the nexus.

Some SDGs are very resource-related in their targets and achievements.

SDG Goal 1, on Ending Poverty

Resource governance is needed to promote equal rights to economic resources, access to basic social goods, ownership and control of land

and other natural resources.

Goal 2, on Ending hunger, achieve food security and promote sustainable Agriculture

Goal 5, on Achieving gender equality and empowerment of women and girls

Critical resources and financing as a force in governance

1. Internal availability/unavailability of marketable material resources as affecting policy choices.

The extensive use of resources in production processes and consumption patterns is a very decisive aspect within the interaction of economic, social, climatic, and environmental changes[50]. For the interlinkages, this is very critical

2. Internal availability/unavailability of human resources as affecting policy choices

3. Internal and external financing possibilities

Connecting these resource issues with other relevant policy areas, such as economic, financial, fiscal or industrial policy, with more intensity on the resources issue within the SDG implementation process will promote social good and sustainable development.

Regrettably, in Nigeria and many other African states, abundance of, and the exploitation of natural resources constitute threat to peace and development. 40% of civil wars in Africa come from the mismanagement of natural resources[51].

---

50 Dittrich, M., Giljum, S., and Polzin, C. Green Economies around the world? The Role of Resources Use for the Development and the Environment. Vienna and Heidelberg: Seri, 2012.
51 Sylvester Bongani Maphosa, Natural Resources and Conflict: Unlocking the

Sufficient attention needs to be paid to the potentials for the mobilisation of internal resources to address development, peace/security, humanitarian and human rights issues. Efficient generation and utilisation of internal resources would make foreign aid and technical assistance superfluous. This would demand the deployment of more efficient methods of the review of budgetary allocations as well as addressing the inadequacies and gaps in implementation.

Increase in financing support equally presented challenges in terms of transparency, accountability, coordination and policy coherence. Special attention needs to be given to ensure that resources provided are aligned with nexus priorities.

Some donor funding does not encourage country-level prioritisation and coordination for effecting the quadruple nexus, with rigid external interest.

Covid-19 teaches the interconnectedness of States as well as situational quadruple nexus. The well-being of our neighbours is the well-being of our own people or nation. The COVID-19 pandemic threatened and continues to threaten everyone with its spread from developed nations, to developing ones.

For Nigeria and many other African countries, the already rickety healthcare systems, poverty, inadequate access to sanitary facilities and practices such as handwashing facilities, awareness, as well as malnutrition and other factors that do threaten or compromise immune systems have resulted in grave consequences. The SDG 3 on good health and wellbeing is threatened with the inadequate and overstretched health facilities. There is also a worsening situation of attention to other diseases, including mental health. The Covid-19 pandemic did not only reveal inefficiencies and failures in governments and institutions but was also a wake-up call

---

economic dimension of peace-building in Africa. Policy Brief, Africa Institute of South Africa. Brief No.74. March 2012.

for governments and societies in general[52]. Governments and societies saw how vulnerable, weak, and threatened their healthcare systems and capacity to handle emergencies were.

The implementation of the nexus approach is not without its challenges and limitations.

- The lack of engagement of civil society could be ameliorated through a focus on this issue within institutional concerns under the situational foundation concern.

- Absence of a common and agreed understanding of problems and by extension conceptualisation.

- Lack of alignment of plans by implementers so as to allow expected synergistic efforts

- Systematic implementation of this new way of working is still at an infancy stage.

The fear that mixing humanitarian, human rights, peace, and development activities will politicize humanitarianism.[53]

---

52 Interview with ECCAS official, December 11, 2020
53 Some of these received mention by the International Council of Voluntary Agencies, Learning livestream

Chapter Three

Survey Report on Situational Quadruple Nexus in Nigeria

The survey as designed was to tease out the views of Nigerians on the interconnectedness of the quadruple nexus within the situational foundation of governance, external dynamics, institutions and resources in the country. The descriptive outcome of the extracted specificity on Nigeria is the following.

Section A. Socio-demographic Characteristics of Respondents

Section A, dealt with the socio-demographic characteristics of the respondents, the sex, age, marital status, as well as the highest educational qualification obtained, and sector, of the respondents were ascertained in this section.

Table 1: Socio-demographic characteristics of the respondents

Variable	Frequency	Percentage
Sex		
Male	133	64.3
Female	74	35.7
Total	**207**	**100**

Age category		
18-27	34	16.4
28-37	79	38.2
38-47	57	27.5
48-57	17	8.2
58 and Above	20	9.7
Total	**207**	**100**

Marital Status		
Divorced	1	0.5
Married	122	58.9
Separated	1	0.5
Single	82	39.6
Widowed	1	0.5
Total	**207**	**100**

Educational Qualification		
Post tertiary education	134	64.7
Tertiary education	68	32.9
Secondary education	5	2.4
Total	**207**	**100**

Sector		
Public government sector	122	58.9
Non State/Private Sector	62	30
Regional/International Institution	23	11.1
Total	**207**	**100**

Specific Sector		
Academic/Media	82	39.6
Development	26	12.6
Legal/Human Rights	9	4.3
NGO/Humanitarian work	41	19.8
Private work	44	21.3
Regional/International work	5	2.4
Total	**207**	**100**

Prevalence of Conflicts in Nigeria		
Highly prevalent	134	64.7
Prevalent	5	2.4
Not prevalent	68	32.9
Total	**207**	**100**

Source: field survey, 2020

Table 1 presents the socio-demographic characteristics of the respondents, the data shows that 64.3% of the respondents are male; 35.7% of the respondents are female. The distribution of the respondents according to their age category shows that 16.4% of the respondents are within the age bracket of 18-27years, 38.2% are within the age bracket of 28-37years, 27.5% of the respondents are within the age bracket of 38-47years, 8.2% of the respondents are within the age bracket of 48-57years while 9.7%

of the respondents are within the age bracket of 58years old and above. This is an indication that a higher percentage (38.2%) of the respondents are within the age bracket of 28-37years. The preponderance of this age category could be explained by the fact that this age category is tech-savvy and since the data was collected online, this age category is more inclined to technology and could easily participate in the survey without any hindrance than the older age category.

The marital status of the respondents shows that 0.5% of the respondents are divorced, 58.9% are married, 0.5% of the respondents are separated, 39.6% of the respondents are single, 0.5% of the respondents are widowed, this shows that the majority (58.9%) of the respondents are married. The distribution of the respondents according to their educational qualification shows that 64.7% of the respondents have a post-tertiary educational qualification, 32.9% have tertiary educational qualification while 2.4% of the respondents have secondary school educational qualification, this implies that majority (64.7%) of the respondents have post-tertiary educational qualification (which includes masters, post-graduate diploma, , masters of philosophy and doctor of philosophy) as their highest level of educational qualification. This has positive implication for awareness and knowledge on the current situation of peace, security, development, human rights and humanitarian pillars in Nigeria.

The distribution of the respondents according to their sector shows that 58.9% of the respondents are in the public government sector, 30% of the respondents are in Non-State sector; 11.1% of the respondents are in the Regional/International sector, this shows that majority of the respondents work in the public government sector. With reference to their specific sector, the data shows that 39.6% of the respondents works in the academic/media sector, 12.6% works in the development sector, 4.3% work in the legal/human right sector, 19.8% work in NGO/Humanitarian sector, 21.3% work in private sector while 2.4% of the respondents works in regional/international sector, this shows that higher percentage of the respondents works in the academic/media sector. The distribution of the respondents according to their rating of the prevalence of conflicts in Nigeria, the result shows that 64.7% of the respondents said that conflicts in Nigeria is highly prevalent, 2.4% said it is prevalent while 32.9% of the respondents were of the opinion that conflicts is not prevalent in Nigeria, this shows that majority of the respondents (64.7%) said that conflicts are prevalent in Nigeria.

Figure 1: A bar chart showing gender distribution of the respondents

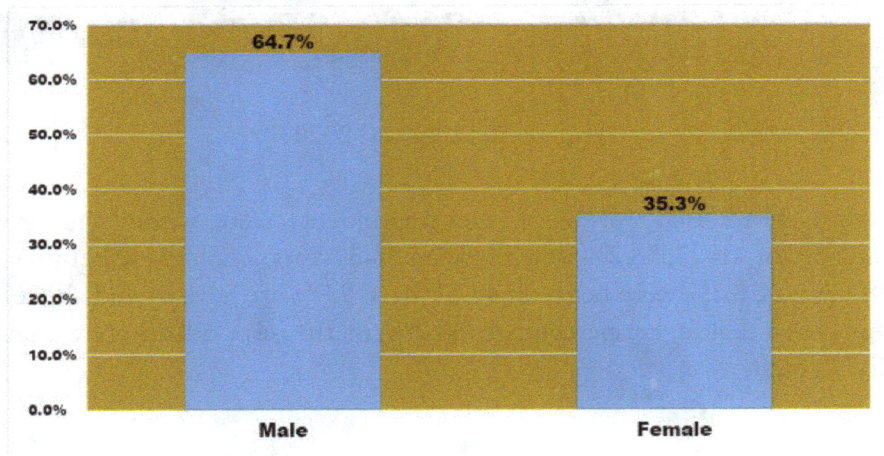

Source: field survey, 2020

Figure 1 above a bar chart showing gender distribution of the respondents, the result shows that 64.7% of the respondents are male while 35.3% of the respondents are female. This shows that the majority of the respondents in the study were male.

Figure 2: A bar chart distribution of respondents according to age category

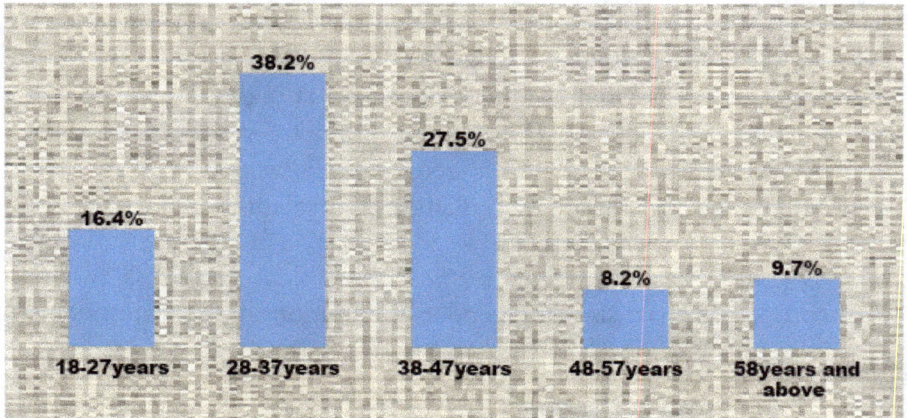

Source: field survey, 2020

Figure shows that 16.4% of the respondents were within the age category of 18-27; 38.2% were between 28-37years, 27.5% were between 38-47years, 8.2% were between 48-57years, 9.7% are 58years and above, this shows that higher percentage (38.2%) of the respondents are within 28-37years.

Figure 3: A Pie chart showing respondents educational qualification

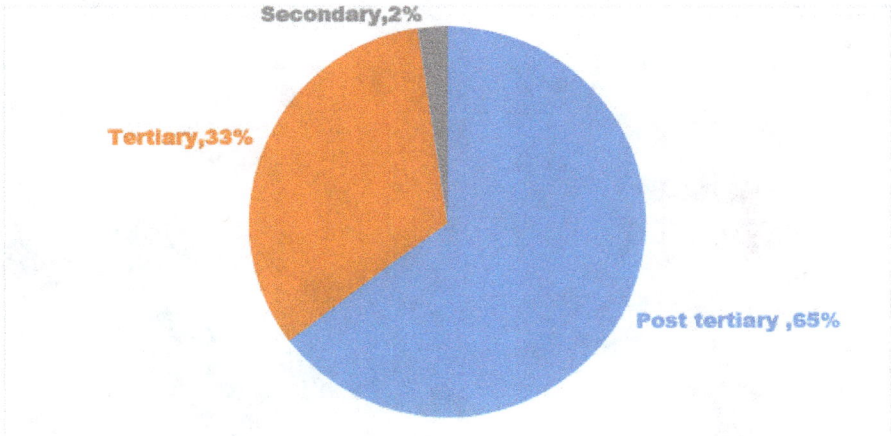

Source: field survey, 2020

Figure 3 is a pie chart showing the distribution of the respondents according to their educational qualifications. The result shows that 33% of the respondents had tertiary educational qualification, 2% had secondary school education while 65% had post tertiary education, this shows that the majority of the respondents had post tertiary education.

Figure 4: A bar chart showing the distribution of respondents on the prevalence of violent conflict, tension and protracted conflicts in Nigeria

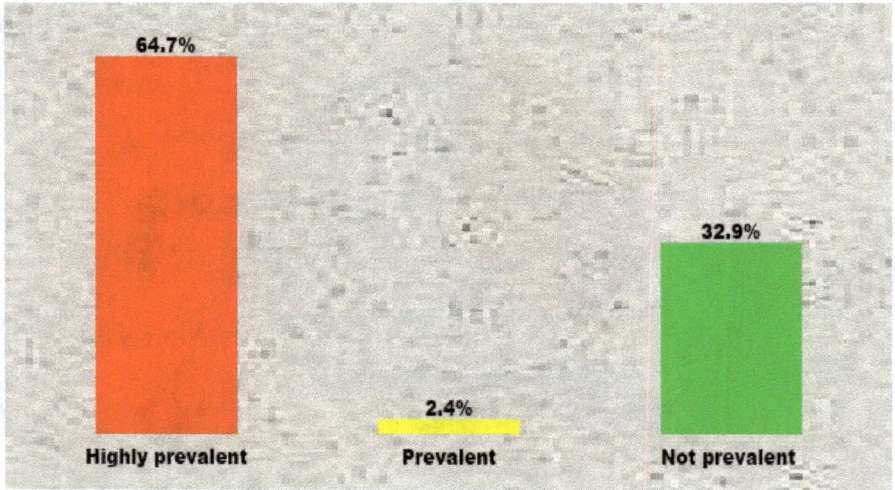

Source: field survey, 2020

Figure 4 is a bar chart showing the distribution of respondents on the prevalence of violent conflict, tension and protracted conflict in Nigeria. The result shows that 64.7% of the respondents said that it is highly prevalent, 2.4% said it is prevalent while 32.9% of respondents said violent conflict, tension and protracts are not prevalent in Nigeria. This implies that the majority (64.7%) of the respondents are of the opinion that violent conflict, tension and protracted conflict is prevalent in Nigeria.

Table 2: Respondents opinion on the prevention and resolution approaches employed in Nigeria to tackle these conflicts

Prevention and Resolution approaches employed	Frequency	Percentage
No prevention and resolution approaches in Nigeria	46	22.2
"Cosmetic resolution" approaches that does not aim at solving the conflicts	22	10.6
Deployment of the military/security agents	29	14
Dialogue and negotiations	5	2.4
Advocacy on peace building	3	1.4
Amnesty programs	7	3.4
Early warning response mechanism	4	2
None, rather government deploys military and security personnel to intimidate the general populace	33	15.9
No effective approach	28	13.5
Placement of curfew are the most prevalent government approach towards tackling conflicts	20	9.7
Reconciliation, community conflict management/arbitration	7	3.4
Forum for post-crisis and inter-community reconciliation	3	1.4
Total	**207**	**100**

Source: field survey, 2020

Table 2 presents respondents opinion on the prevention and resolution approaches employed in Nigeria, The result shows that 22.2% of the respondents were of the opinion that there was no prevention and resolution approaches in Nigeria; 10.6% said that it was "cosmetic resolution" approaches that does not aim at solving the conflicts; 14% of the respondents were of the opinion that deployment of the military/ security agents were the prevention and resolution approaches employed in Nigeria to tackle these conflicts; 2.4% said it was dialogue and negotiations; 1.4% said advocacy on peace building was the prevention and resolution approaches employed in Nigeria to tackle these conflicts; while 3.4% said it is through amnesty programs; 2% said it is through early warning response mechanism; 15.9% said there was no prevention and resolution mechanism rather the government deploys military and security personnel to intimidate the general approaches; 13.5% said there was no effective approach employed in Nigeria; 9.7% of the respondents said placement of curfew are the most prevalent government approaches towards tackling conflicts; Furthermore, 3.4% of the respondents were of the opinion that reconciliation, community conflict management/ arbitration were the approaches employed in Nigeria to prevent and resolve conflicts; 1.4% of the respondents were of the opinion that forum for post-crisis and inter-community reconciliation were the prevention and resolution approaches employed in Nigeria.

Section B: Peace and Security in Nigeria

This section dealt with peace and security threats in Nigeria, rating of peace and security by the respondents, factors underlying peace and security threats in Nigeria, how Covid-19 Pandemic affected safety and security among other cogent issues that were analyzed in this section.

Figure 5: A bar chart showing respondents rating of peace and security in Nigeria

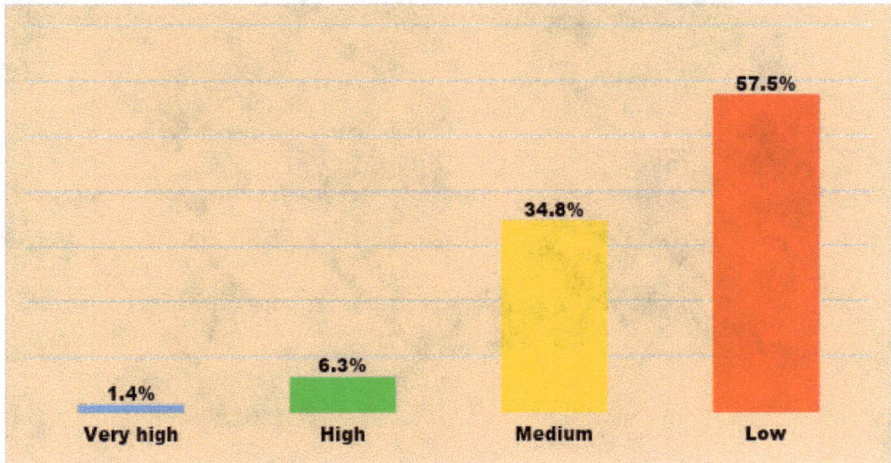

Source: field survey, 2020

Figure 5 is a bar chart showing respondents rating of peace and security in Nigeria, the result shows that 1.4% of the respondents stated that peace and security is very high in Nigeria, 6.3% of the respondents said peace and security is high, 34.8% said peace and security is medium in Nigeria while 57.5% of the respondents were of the opinion that peace and security is low in Nigeria. This is an indication that there is a low level of peace and security in Nigeria.

Figure 6: A bar chart showing major threats to peace and security in Nigeria according to the respondents

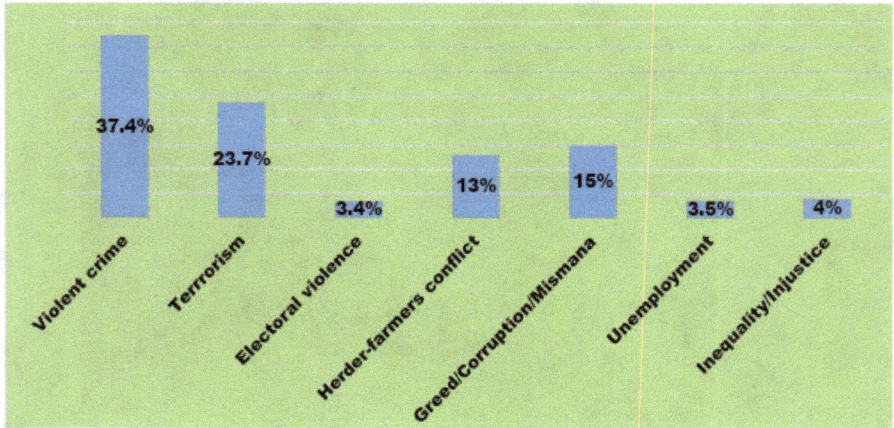

Source: field survey, 2020

Figure 6 above presents respondents opinion on threats to peace and security in Nigeria according to the respondents, the result shows that 37.4% of the respondents are of the opinion that violent crime is one of the threats to peace and security in Nigeria, 23.7% said it is terrorism, 3.4% said it is electoral violence, 13% said it is herders-farmers conflict, 15% said it is greed/corruption and mismanagement, 3.5% said it is unemployment while 4% said it is inequality and injustice. This shows that there are several threats to peace and security in Nigeria.

Table 3: Respondents opinion on the prevalence of the identified threats to peace and security in Nigeria

Peace and security threats that are more prevalent in Nigeria		
Peace and security threats in Nigeria	**Frequency**	**Percentages**
Terrorism	56	27.1
Armed robbery	19	9.2
Banditry	17	8.2
Kidnapping	20	9.7
Human rights abuse	11	5.3
Cattle rustling	9	4.3
Farmer-herder conflict	23	11.1
Corruption	32	15.5
Electoral violence	5	2.4
Police brutality	15	7.2
Total	**207**	**100%**

Source: field survey, 2020

Table 3 above presents respondents' opinions on peace and security threats that are more prevalent in Nigeria. The result shows that 27.1% of the respondents were of the view that that terrorism is more prevalent, 9.2% said it is armed robbery, 8.2% said it is banditry, 9.7% said it is kidnapping, 5.3% said it is human rights abuse, 4.3% of the respondents said cattle rustling is more prevalent in Nigeria, 11.1% of the respondents said farmer-herder conflict is prevalent, 15.5% of the respondents said that corruption is more prevalent in Nigeria, 2.4% of the respondents said electoral violence is more prevalent while 7.2% of the respondents said police brutality is more prevalent in Nigeria. This shows that higher percentage (27.1%) of the respondents said that terrorism is more prevalent in Nigeria.

This could be as a result of unrelenting strikes and attacks by the Boko Haram insurgent.

Figure 7: Respondents' opinions on factors that promote/encourage threats to peace and security in Nigeria

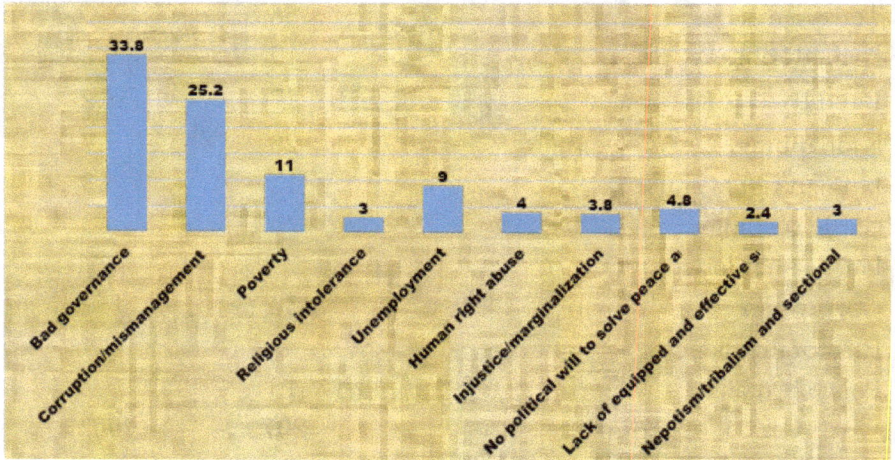

Source: field survey, 2020

Figure 7 presents respondents opinion on factors that promote/ encourages the threats to peace and security in Nigeria, the result shows that 33.8% of the respondents said bad governance encourages peace and security threats in Nigeria, 25.2% said that corruption and mismanagement encourages threats to peace and security in Nigeria, 11% said it is poverty, 3% said it is religious intolerance, 9% said it is unemployment, 4% said it is human right abuse, 3.8% said it is injustice/ marginalisation, 4.8% said lack of political will to solve peace and security problem encourages threats to peace and security in Nigeria, 2.4% of the respondents said lack of equipped and effective security personnel encourages threats to peace and security while 3% said it is nepotism, tribalism and sectionalism. This shows that a higher percentage (33.8%)

of the respondents opined that bad governance encourages peace and security threats in Nigeria.

Figure 8: Respondents opinion on whether Covid-19 pandemic affected their safety and security

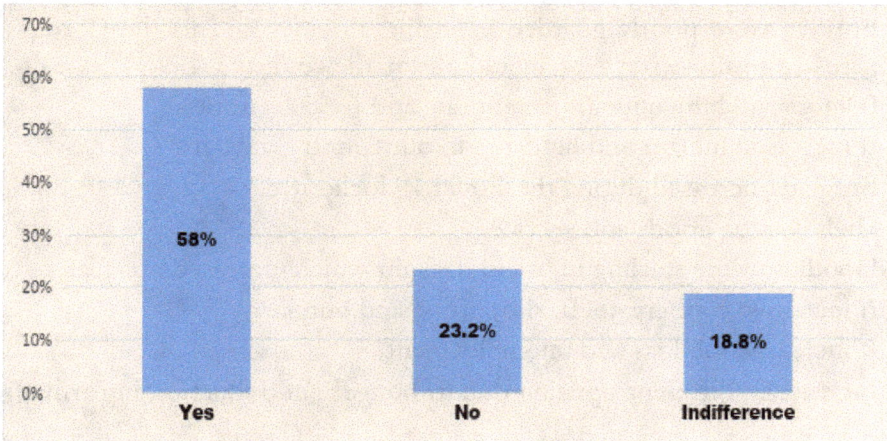

Source: field survey, 2020

Figure 8 presents respondent's opinion on whether Covid-19 pandemic affected their safety and security, the result shows that 58% of the respondents said yes that Covid-19 pandemic affected their safety and security, 23.2% of the respondents said no that Covid-19 pandemic affected their safety and security, while 18.8% of the respondents are indifference. This shows that the majority (58%) of the respondents said that Covid-19 affected their safety and security.

Table 4: Respondents opinion on how they were affected by Covid-19

Covid-19 lockdown aggravated poverty which led to crime and insecurity

The Covid-19 lockdown caused an increase in crime rate and insecurity as people tried to survive by all means

Borders were poorly guarded exposing all cities and to the Corona Virus from those traveling in and out of the country

It aggravated the unemployment rate and food security

It increased hunger and hardship in our country

Burglary increased during the Covid-19 lockdown

High cost of goods and services

Hoodlum were stealing in broad daylight which increased our fear

It increased robbery, theft, shoplifting and burglary

It increased job loss and unemployment

Increase in different uprising due to hunger and reduction in earning power

Extortion and brutality from security agents enforcing the Covid-19 lockdown

Shut down of the economic, religious and educational sector which led to high rate of crime

Source: field survey, 2020

Table 4 shows the specific ways Covid-19 affected respondents' safety and security. From the table, it was glaring that the Covid-19 lockdown led to increased crime rate which affected the respondents' safety and security in diverse forms.

Table 5: Respondents' opinion on whether the fear of the police force and other security agents is a major concern in Nigeria

Is fear of the police force and other security agents a major concern in Nigeria?		
Responses	**Frequency**	**Percentages**
Yes	132	63.8
No	46	22.2
Indifference	29	14
Total	**207**	**100**

Source: field survey, 2020

Table 5 presents respondents' opinion on whether the fear of the police force, and other security agencies is a major concern in Nigeria, the result shows that 63.8% of the respondents said yes that the fear of police and other security agents is a major concern in Nigeria, 22.2% said no that the fear of police and other security agents is not a concern in Nigeria while 14% of the respondents were indifference to the question whether the fear of the police and other security agents is a major concern in Nigeria. This is an indication that the majority (63.8%) of the respondents stated that the fear of the police force and other security agents is a major concern in Nigeria. This could be as a result of police brutality, extortion and harassment, as we will see in the next table.

Table 6A: Respondents opinion on why they are afraid of the Police and other security agents in Nigeria

Extra-judicial killings
Arbitrary arrest and extortion by the Police
Human rights violations by the Police and other security agents
Police and other security agents act with impunity and have no regard for rule of law
Police "frame-up" innocent citizens just to extort money from them
High level of corruption in the police, they can do anything to get money
High handedness of the police
They are brutal and uses excessive force/violence
Innocent citizens are profiled as criminals to extort money from them
The police harass innocent citizens at will
The police don't have respect for human life
Because the police are armed, they can shoot innocent citizens and nothing will happen to them
They are lawless and easily get away with crime committed against innocent citizens
They are more dangerous than the terrorists due to their unprofessional behaviour and wickedness

Source: field survey, 2020

Table 6A showcases reasons why respondents are afraid of the police and other security agents in Nigeria, the reasons include police brutality, extortion, arbitrary arrest, extra-judicial killings, lack of respect for human rights, and human life in Nigeria.

Table 6B: Respondents' opinion on whether corruption and lack of transparency are the greatest threat to achieving peace and security in Nigeria

Are corruption and lack of transparency the greatest threat to achieving peace and security?		
Responses	**Frequency**	**Percentages**
Strongly agree	144	69.6
Agree	45	21.7
Neither agree nor disagree	16	7.7
Disagree	2	1
Total	**207**	**100%**

Source: field survey, 2020

Table 6B presents respondents' opinion on whether corruption and lack of transparency are the greatest threat to achieving peace and security, the result shows that 69.6% of the respondents agreed that corruption and lack of transparent are the greatest threat to achieving peace and security, 21.7% of the respondents agreed that lack of transparency is the greatest threat to achieving peace and security, 7.7% of the respondents neither agree nor disagree that lack of transparency is the greatest threat to achieving peace and security while 1% of the respondents disagreed that lack of transparency is the greatest threat to achieving peace and security, this implies that majority (69.6%) of the respondents strongly agreed that corruption and transparency are the greatest threat to achieving peace and security in Nigeria.

Table 7: Respondents' opinion on how many times them or their household have been a victim of insecurity in the past 12months preceding this study

How many times have they or their household been a victim of insecurity in the past 12 months preceding this study?		
Responses	**Frequency**	**Percentages**
None	48	23.2
Once	56	27
Twice	40	19.3
Thrice	22	10.6
Four-Ten times	17	8.2
Over ten times	11	5.3
Often	13	6.3
Total	**207**	**100%**

Source: field survey, 2020

Table 7 above shows respondents' response on how many times them or their household have been a victim of insecurity in the past 12months preceding this study, the result shows that 23.2% of the respondent said them nor their household have not been victims of insecurity in the past 12months preceding this study, 27% said they have been victim once, 19.3% said they have been victims twice, 10.6% said they have been victims thrice, 8.2% of the respondents said they have been victims of insecurity within 4-10times in the past 12months preceding this study, 5.3% said they have been victims over ten times, 6.3% said they have been victim often.

Figure 9: Respondents' opinion on how often people suffer loss of properties, assets or investments as a result of insecurity issues in Nigeria

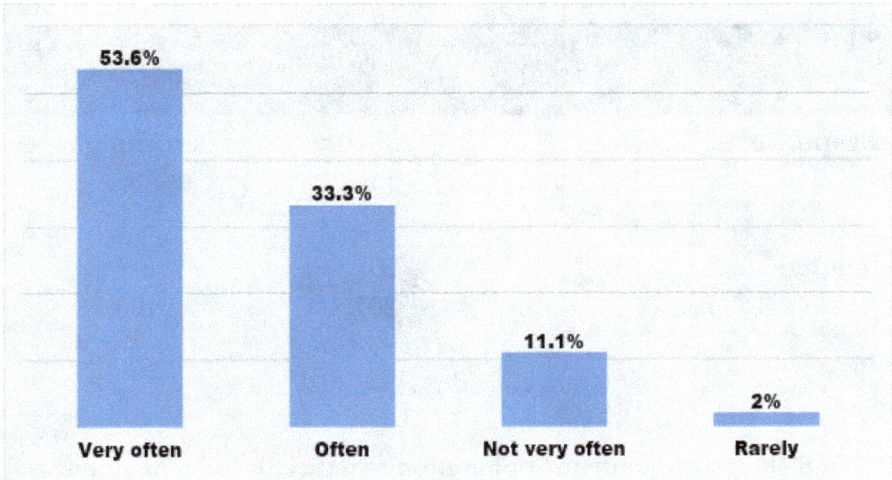

Source: field survey, 2020

Figure 9 above presents respondents' opinion on how often people suffer loss of properties, assets or investments as a result of insecurity in Nigeria. The result shows that 53.6% of the respondents said that people suffer loss of properties, assets or investments as a result of insecurity issues in Nigeria very often, 33.3% said people suffer loss of properties, assets or investments as a result of insecurity issues in Nigeria often, 11.1% said it is not often while 2% of the respondents said that people rarely suffer loss of properties, assets or involvement as a result of insecurity in Nigeria. This shows that the majority (53.6%) of the respondents opined that people suffer loss of properties, assets or investments as a result of insecurity in Nigeria.

Table 8: Respondents' opinion on whether the fear of crime and insecurity affect business activities in Nigeria

Is the fear of crime and insecurity affecting business activities in Nigeria?		
Response	**Frequency**	**Percentages**
Yes	178	86
No	11	5.3
Indifferent	18	8.7
Total	**207**	**100**

Source: field survey, 2020

Table 8 shows respondents' opinion on whether the fear of crime and insecurity affect business activities in Nigeria. The result shows that 86% of the respondents said yes, that the fear of crime and insecurity affect business activities in Nigeria, 5.3% of the respondents said no that the fear of crime and insecurity does not affect business activities in Nigeria, while 8.7% of the respondents were indifferent to whether the fear of crime and insecurity affect business activities in Nigeria. This implies that the majority (86%) of the respondents said yes that fear of crime and insecurity affect business activities in Nigeria.

Figure 10: Respondents opinion on how much they trust the state security system in Nigeria

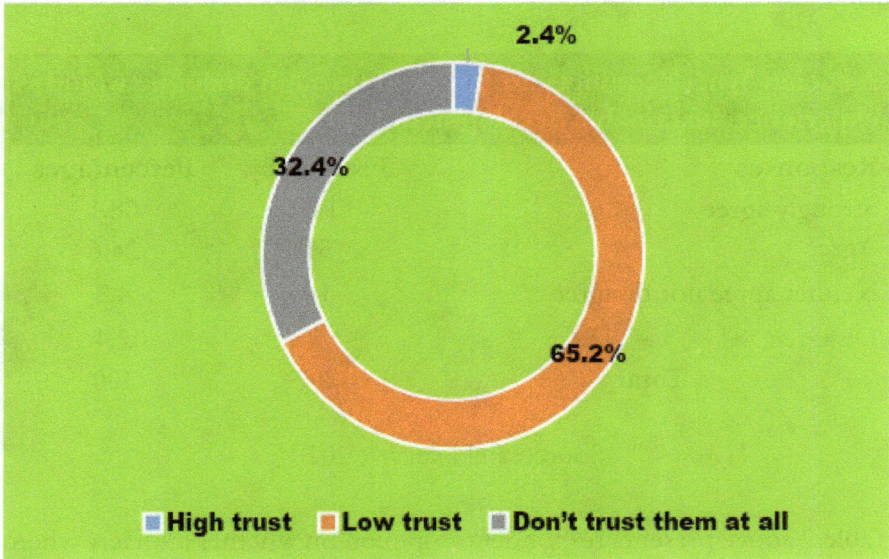

Source: field survey, 2020

Figure 10 presents respondents' opinions on how much they trust the state security system. The result shows that 2.4% of the respondents said they have high trust for the state security system in Nigeria, 65.2% of the respondents said they have low trust in the state security system in Nigeria while 32.4% of the respondents said they do not trust the state security system in Nigeria at all. This shows that the majority (65.2%) of the respondents have low trust in the state security system in Nigeria. This could be as a result of the inefficiency of the state security system in Nigeria to curtail and control insecurity, violent crimes, and conflict in Nigeria.

Table 9: Respondents' opinion on whether a society where conflicts are resolved through dialogue would experience sustainable development faster

A society where conflicts are resolved through dialogue would experience sustainable development faster?		
Responses	**Frequency**	**Percentages**
Strongly agree	141	68.1
Agree	51	24.6
Neither agree nor disagree	10	4.8
Disagree	5	2.4
Total	**207**	**100**

Source: field survey, 2020

Table 9 above presents respondents' opinion on whether a society where conflicts are resolved through dialogue would experience sustainable development faster, the result shows that 68.1% of the respondents strongly agree that a society where conflicts are resolved through dialogue would experience sustainable development faster, 24.6% of the respondents agree that a society where conflicts are resolved through dialogue would experience sustainable development faster, 4.8% of the respondents neither agree nor disagree that a society where conflicts are resolved through dialogue would experience sustainable development faster while 2.4% of the respondents disagree that a society where conflicts are resolved through dialogue would experience sustainable development faster. This implies that the majority (68.1%) of the respondents strongly agreed that a society where conflicts are resolved through dialogue would experience sustainable development faster.

Figure 11: Respondents' opinion on whether religious intolerance is a major threat to peace and security in Nigeria

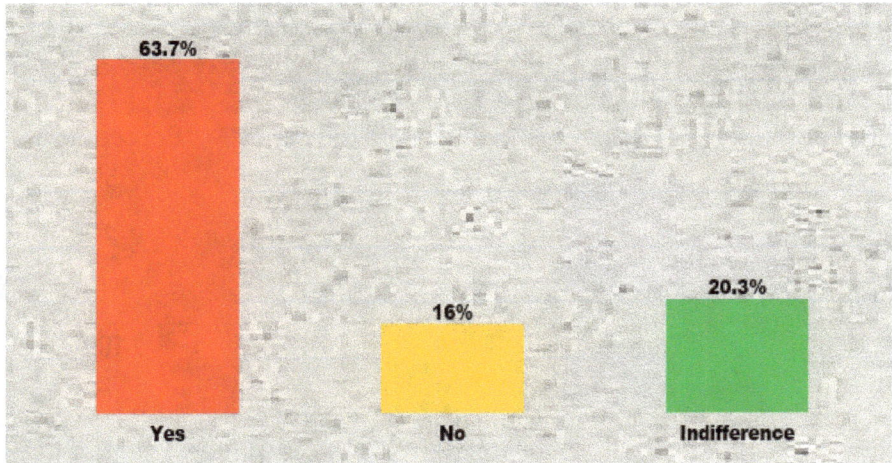

Source: field survey, 2020

Figure 11 above shows respondents' opinion on whether religious intolerance is a major threat to peace and security in Nigeria, the result shows that 63.7% of the respondents said yes that religious intolerance is a major threat to peace and security in Nigeria, 16% of the respondents said no that religious intolerance is not a major threat to peace and security in Nigeria, while 20.3% of the respondents where indifferent on whether religious intolerance is a major threat to peace and security in Nigeria, this implies that majority (63.7%) of the respondents said yes that religious intolerance is a major threat to peace and security in Nigeria.

Table 10: Respondents' opinion on whether lack of good governance in Nigeria hinder the existence of peace and security?

Does lack of good governance in Nigeria hinder the existence of peace and security?		
Responses	**Frequency**	**Percentages**
Strongly agree	122	59
Agree	74	35.7
Neither agree nor disagree	9	4.3
Disagree	2	1
Total	**207**	**100**

Source: field survey, 2020

Table 10 presents respondents' opinion on whether lack of good governance in Nigeria hinder the existence of peace and security, the result shows that 59% of the respondents, 35.7% of the respondents agree that lack of good governance in Nigeria hinders the existence of peace and security, 4.3% of the respondents neither agree nor disagree that lack of good governance in Nigeria hinder the existence of peace and security while 1% of the respondents disagree that lack of good governance in Nigeria hinder the existence of peace and security, this is an indication that majority (59%) of the respondents strongly agree that lack of good governance in Nigeria hinder the existence of peace and security.

Figure 12: Respondents' opinion on whether ethnic marginalisation and grievance account for violent conflict in Nigeria?

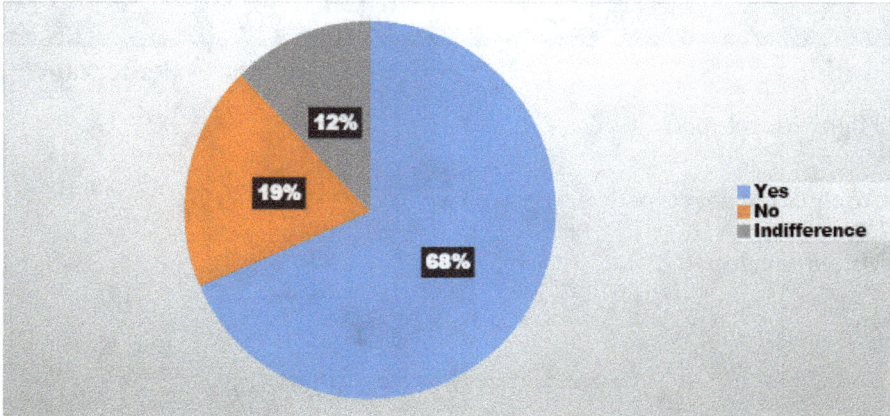

Source: field survey, 2020

Figure 12 above shows respondents' opinion on whether ethnic marginalisation and grievance account for violent conflict in Nigeria, the result shows that 69% of the respondents said yes that ethnic marginalisation and grievance account for violent conflict in Nigeria, 12% of the respondents said no that ethnic marginalisation and grievance does not account for violent conflict in Nigeria, while 19% of the respondents were indifferent on whether ethnic marginalisation and grievance account for violent conflict in Nigeria. This implies that ethnic marginalisation and grievance account for violent conflicts in Nigeria.

Section C: Development.

This section focused on developmental issues within Nigeria. Respondents were asked to rate the level of development in Nigeria, factors they think hinders development in Nigeria, amongst other vital issues. Their responses and opinions are presented below in the form of charts and tables.

Table 11: Respondents' rating of developmental level in Nigeria?

How do you rate the level of development in Nigeria?		
Ratings	**Frequency**	**Percentages**
Highly developed	3	1.4
Adequately developed	16	7.7
Underdeveloped	188	90.8%
Total	**207**	**100%**

Source: field survey, 2020

Table 11 above presents how respondents rate the level of development in Nigeria, the data shows that 1.4% of the respondents rated Nigeria as highly developed, 7.7% rated Nigeria as adequately developed while 90.8% of the respondents rated Nigeria as underdeveloped. This is the implication that the majority (91.5%) rated Nigeria as underdeveloped. This could be as a result of infrastructural deficit, bad governance, lack of basic social amenities, lack of health and educational facilities in Nigeria.

Figure 13: Respondents' opinion on what they think hinders development in Nigeria.

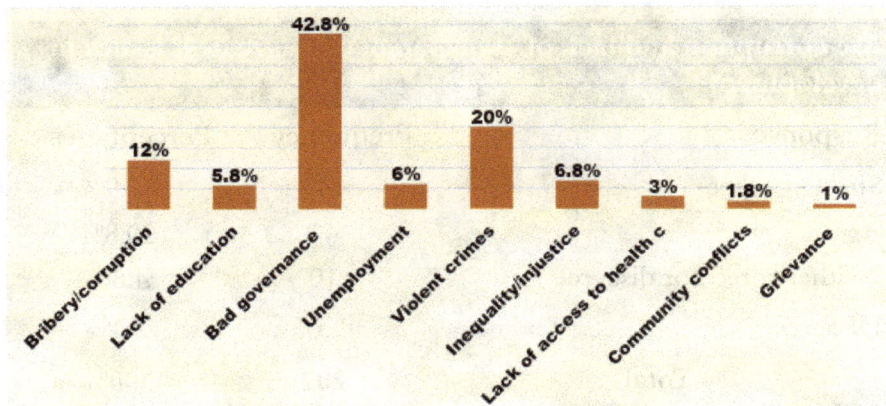

Source: field survey, 2020

Figure 13 presents respondents' opinion on what they think hinders development in Nigeria, the result shows that 12% of the respondents opined that bribery/corruption were the major hindrance to development in Nigeria, 5.8% said that lack of education is the major hindrance to development, 42.8% of the respondents opined that bad governance is the major hindrance to development in Nigeria, 6% of the respondents stated that unemployment is the major hindrance to development in Nigeria, 20% of the respondents stated that violent crimes is the major hindrance to development in Nigeria, 6.8% of the respondents stated that inequality/injustice is the major hindrance to development in Nigeria, 3% of the respondents were of the opinion that lack of access to health is the major hindrance to development in Nigeria, 1.8% of the respondents stated that community conflict is the major hindrance to development in Nigeria, while 1% of the respondent stated that grievance is the major hindrance to development in Nigeria. This implies that bad governance is one of the major hindrances to development in Nigeria.

Table 12: Respondents' opinion on whether corruption and lack of transparency are the greatest issues in development

Are corruption and lack of transparency the greatest issues in development?		
Responses	**Frequency**	**Percentages**
Strongly agree	149	71.9%
Agree	43	20.8%
Neither agree nor disagree	10	4.8%
Disagree	5	2.4%
Total	**207**	**100%**

Source: field survey, 2020

Table 12 above presents respondents' opinion on whether corruption and lack of transparency are the greatest issues in development, the data shows that 71.9% of the respondents are strongly agreed that corruption and lack of transparency are the greatest issues in development, 20.8% agreed that corruption and lack of transparency are the greatest issues in development, 4.8% of the respondents neither agree nor disagree that corruption and lack of transparency are the greatest issues in development, while 2.4% of the respondents disagreed that corruption and lack of transparency are the greatest issues in development. This implies that corruption and lack of transparency in governance are the greatest issues in development.

Table 13: Respondents' opinion on whether ethnic marginalisation and economic deprivation have retarded development in some part of Nigeria

Ethnic marginalisation and economic deprivation have retarded development in some part of Nigeria?		
Ratings	**Frequency**	**Percentages**
Yes	120	57.9%
No	68	32.8%
Indifference	19	9.2%
Total	**207**	**100%**

Source: field survey, 2020

Table 13 presents respondents' opinion on whether ethnic marginalisation and economic deprivation have retarded development in some part of Nigeria, the result shows that 57.9% of the respondents said yes that ethnic marginalisation and economic deprivation have retarded development in some part of Nigeria, 32.8% of the respondents said no that ethnic marginalisation and economic deprivation have not retarded development in some part of their country, while 9.2% of the respondents were indifferent to whether ethnic marginalisation and economic deprivation have retarded development in some part of Nigeria, this implies that ethnic marginalisation and economic deprivation have retarded development in some parts of Nigeria.

Table 14: Respondents' opinion on ethnic groups that are less developed and why they are less developed

Ethnic groups in Eastern Nigeria are extremely underdeveloped whereas minerals and exploration of raw materials take place in the region
The Igbos are marginalised and excluded
The southern Nigeria is marginalised due to ethnic and religious sentiments
Due to favouritism and injustice some ethnic groups are marginalised
Igbos are marginalised because the Buhari led administration said Igbos didn't vote for him
The Niger-Delta are marginalised
The North are marginalised because their leaders hide under Islamic religion practice to subjugate them, making them uneducated and dysfunctional
The south south ethnic groups are marginalised despite being responsible for the greater portion of national income and foreign exchange earnings
The southern regions are backward because of the corruption of their leaders
The south-south is seeking for resource control and that is why they are still underdeveloped
Those in power favour their own ethnic groups/community and religion

Source: field survey, 2020

Table 14 presents respondents' opinions on which ethnic group is less developed and why they are less developed, the result shows that marginalisation, injustice, favouritism, social exclusion are the major reasons why some ethnic groups are less developed. The Igbos of southeast and other ethnic groups in South-South Nigeria are also widely marginalised.

Figure 14: Respondents' opinion on whether poor people around them have access to education in Nigeria.

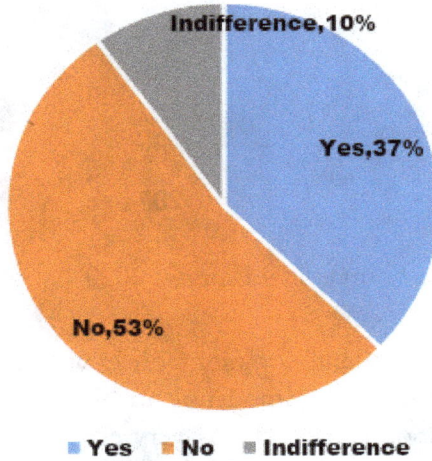

Source: field survey, 2020

Figure 14 is a pie chart showing respondents' opinion on whether poor people around them have access to education in Nigeria, the result shows that 37.2% of the respondents said yes that poor people around them have access to education in Nigeria, 52.9% of the respondents said no that poor people around them do not have access to education in Nigeria, while 10% if the respondents were indifferent on whether poor people around them have access to education in Nigeria, this shows that poor people in Nigeria do not have access to education.

Table 15: Respondent's opinion on how difficult it is for the poor to secure a modest accommodation in Nigeria.

How difficult is it for the poor to secure modest accommodation in Nigeria		
Ratings	Frequency	Percentages
Very easy	16	7.7%
Easy	10	4.8%
Difficult	142	68.6%
Very difficult	39	18.8%
Total	207	100%

Source: Field survey, 2020

Table 15 presents respondents' opinions on how difficult it is for the poor to secure a modest accommodation in Nigeria, the result shows that 7.7% of the respondents said it is very easy for the poor around them to secure, 4.8% of the respondents said it is very for the poor to secure a modest accommodation in Nigeria, 68.6% said it is difficult for the poor to secure a modest accommodation in Nigeria, 18.8% of the respondents said it is very difficult for poor to secure a modest accommodation in Nigeria, this implies that it is difficult for the poor to secure a modest accommodation in Nigeria.

Figure 15: Respondents' opinion on whether Covid-19 affected their source of livelihood

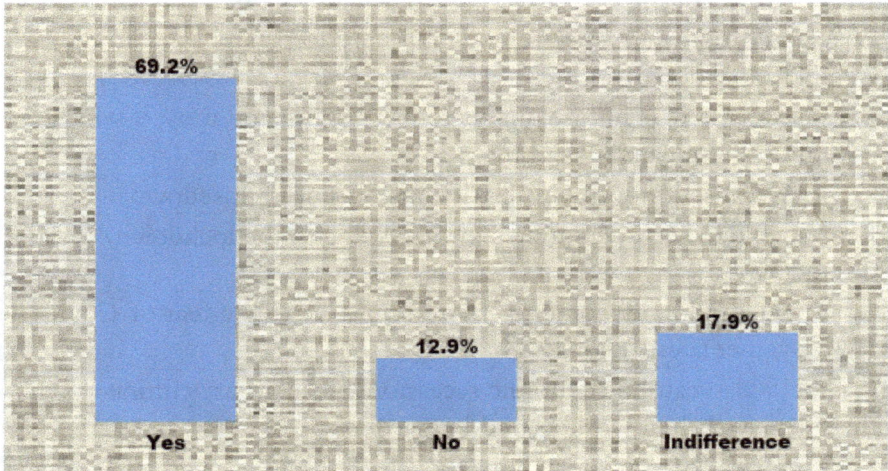

Source: field survey, 2020

Figure 15 is a bar chart showing respondents' reactions on whether Covid-19 affected their source of livelihood, the result shows that 69.2% of the respondents said yes that the Covid-19 affected their means of livelihood, 12.9% of the respondents said no that the Covid-19 did not affect their means of livelihood, while 17.9% of the respondents were indifferent on whether the Covid-19 affected their means of livelihood. This implies that Covid-19 affected the livelihood of a lot of people in Nigeria.

Table 16: Respondents' opinion on how Covid-19 affected their source of livelihood

As a landlord, my tenants are finding it hard to pay rent due to the Covid-19 lockdown
Because so many firms are unable to pay salaries and most workers have no other means of income
Covid-19 caused movement restrictions/business closedown
I am unable to secure contracts/projects due to the lockdown/social distancing
Customers no longer come to shop to buy due to the fear of Covid-19/movement restrictions
Covid-19 also caused economic recessions so firms are cutting down the salaries of their workers and I am affected
Hike in prices of transportation/foodstuff, things are very expensive now in the market
I lost my job during the pandemic because my company were cutting cost by downsizing
As a legal practitioner, I couldn't get clients during those periods and it was difficult to survive
It affected salary payment/business opportunities and transactions
It halted the activities of the agency I work on an ad-hoc basis, thus I lost that source of livelihood
It restricted movement thereby reducing income
My company can no longer pay all the staffs and had to lay off some of us
My salary was slashed by 50%
NGO funded projects were halted and that was my source of livelihood

Source: field survey, 2020

Table 16 shows that Covid-19 affected respondents' means of livelihood in diverse ways, some of the respondents opined that their salaries were slashed by 50%, some of the respondents were laid off, some opined that due to the restriction of movements their businesses were affected which in turn affected their means of livelihood. Landlords and owners of properties stated that their tenants found it difficult to meet their annual rent payments. Many firms, companies, agencies and organisations found it very difficult to pay the salaries of their workers. Some of the respondents could not secure contracts/projects due to the Covid-19 lockdown. Some of the respondents were laid off by their organisations because of downsizing.

Table 17: Respondents' opinion on how Civil Society Organisations promote sustainable development in Nigeria

By giving grants to Small and Medium Enterprises (SMEs)
By coming down to the grassroots where they might be at the first place to checkmate various hardships facing an average man
By engaging the government in accountability and transparency
Advocacy to raise awareness and build the capacity of communities
Enlightenment on participatory development and citizen contributing its own quota in attitude, integrity, value chain addition
By assisting and advising the government on the best development plan to execute
By being accountable to various resources mapped out by the government or other NGOs toward the welfare of the common man whom they represent
By being vigilant in the oversight of government policies and activities
By building community structures to engage in project monitoring
By creating awareness and empowering SMEs
By creating economic empowerment opportunities for the jobless

By dialogue, peacebuilding advocacy, mediation, workshops, skill acquisitions, and empowerment
By directing identifying and executing projects by educating the masses
By giving education and scholarship to indigent children and citizens
By providing grants and loans to the SMEs
CSOs can hold the government accountable by acting as watchdogs to ensure they uphold the rule of law
CSOs can also act as a pressure group to lobby the government to implement the campaign promises that brought them to power

Source: field survey, 2020

Table 17 presents respondents' opinions on how Civil Society Organisations promote sustainable development in their state and country. Respondents expressed their thoughts on what the CSOs should do to promote sustainable development. Majority of the views show that respondents believe there is more that CSOs can do to promote sustainable development. For example, Corporate Social Responsibilities are carried out by the CSOs. From the respondents' opinions, CSOs can promote sustainable development by giving grants to indigenous SMEs and also executing developmental projects at the grassroots. CSOs can also significantly engage and hold the government accountable by pushing for advocacies to raise awareness and build the capacity of communities. CSOs can also promote sustainable development by carrying out enlightenment on participatory development and citizen contribution and ownership of community development through attitudinal change, integrity, and value chain addition. CSOs can also promote sustainable development by creating economic empowerment opportunities., expanding access to education especially through the provision of scholarships to indigent children, especially in rural communities and suburbs.

Section D: Human Rights

Section D was concerned with issues of human rights, respondents were asked to rate the level of respect for human rights in Nigeria, threats to human rights in Nigeria, law enforcement agents, and respect for human rights, amongst other issues. Respondents' reactions are presented in tables and charts below.

Table 18: Respondents' ratings of the level of respect for human rights in Nigeria

How do you rate the level of respect for human rights in Nigeria?		
Ratings	Frequency	Percentages
Very high	2	1
High	14	6.7
Medium	56	27.1
Low	87	42
Very low	48	23.2
Total	**207**	**100%**

Source: field survey, 2020

Table 18 presents respondents' rating of the level of respect for human rights in Nigeria. The result shows that 1% of the respondents rated the level of respect for human rights in Nigeria as very high, 6.7% rated it as high, 27.1% rated it as medium, 42% rated it as low, while 23.2% of the respondents rated the level of respect for human rights in Nigeria as very low. This shows that the level of respect for human rights in Nigeria is very low.

Figure 16: Respondents' opinions on what they consider the greatest threat to human rights in Nigeria.

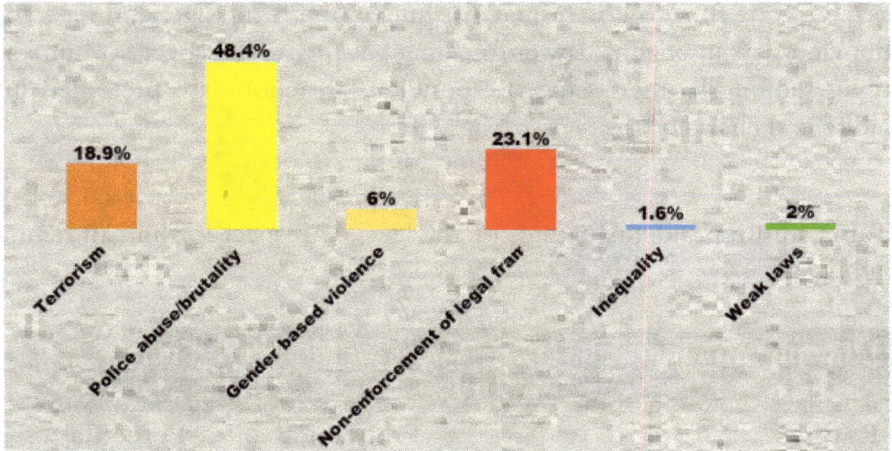

Source: field survey, 2020

Figure 16 above presents respondents' opinion on what they consider the greatest threat to human rights in Nigeria. 18.9% of the respondents believe that terrorism is the greatest threat to human rights in Nigeria. 48.4% of the respondents opined that police abuse/brutality is the greatest threat to human rights in Nigeria. 6% of the respondents were of the opinion that gender-based violence is the greatest threat to human rights in Nigeria. 23.1% of the respondents think non-enforcement of legal framework is the greatest threat to human rights in Nigeria. 1.6% of the respondents were of the opinion that inequality/injustice is the greatest threat to human right in Nigeria, while 2% of the respondents said that weak laws are the major threat to human rights in Nigeria. This implies that police brutality and abuse is the greatest threat to human rights in Nigeria.

Table 19: Respondents' opinions on whether more developed societies with greater respect for human rights have more effective government.

Do more developed societies with greater respect for human rights have more effective governments?		
Responses	**Frequency**	**Percentages**
Strongly agree	139	67.1%
Agree	54	26.1%
Neither agree nor disagree	12	5.8%
Disagree	2	1%
Total	**207**	**100%**

Source: field survey, 2020

Table 19 presents respondents' opinions on whether more developed societies with greater respect for human rights have more effective government. The result shows that 67.1% of the respondents strongly agree to the assertion that developed societies with greater respect for human rights have more effective government, 26.1% agreed, 5.8% of the respondents neither agreed or disagreed. While 1% of the respondents disagreed that more developed societies with greater respect for human rights have more effective government.

83

Figure 17: Respondents' opinions on the seriousness of the human right challenge in Nigeria

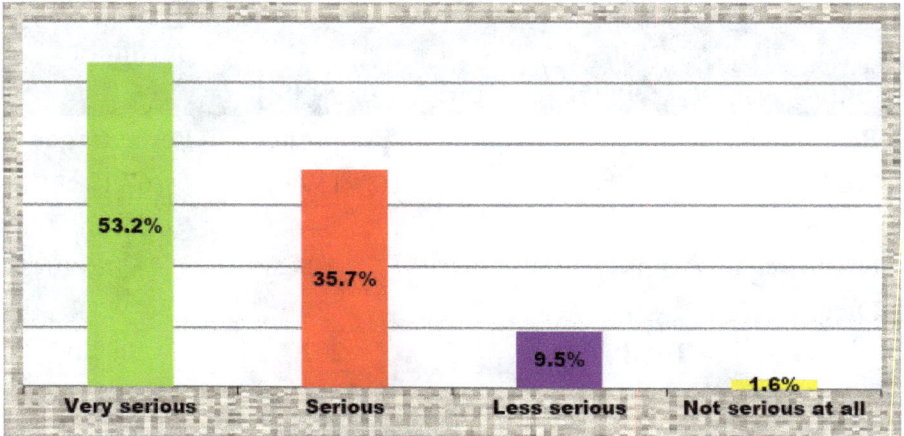

Source: field survey, 2020

Figure 17 presents respondents' opinions on how serious the general human right challenge is in Nigeria. The result shows that 53.2% of the respondents opined that the general human rights challenge is a very serious issue in Nigeria, 35.7% of the respondents said it is serious, 9.5% of the respondents said it is less serious, while 1.6% of the respondents said it is not serious at all. This implies that the general human right challenge in Nigeria is a very serious issue, this could be as a result of extra-judicial killings by security agents, brutality and harassment of the populace in Nigeria.

Figure 18: Respondents' opinions on how free they are to practice any religion of their choice in Nigeria?

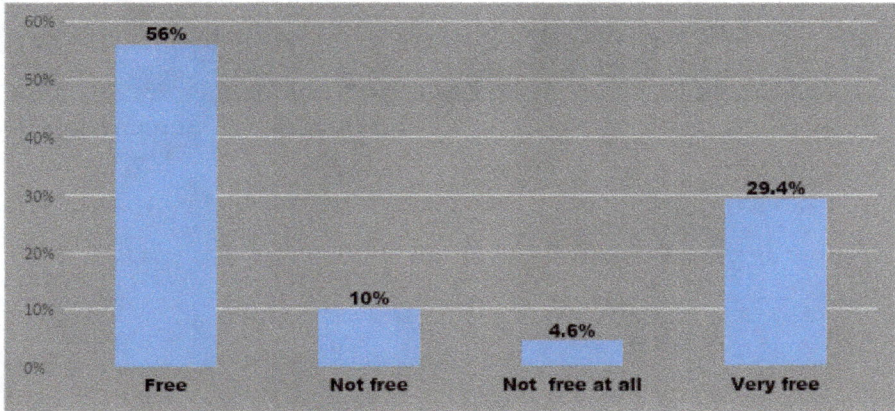

Source: field survey, 2020

Figure 18 is a bar chart showing respondents' opinions on how free they are to practice any religion of their choice in Nigeria. The result shows that 56% of the respondents are of the opinion that they are free to practice any religion of their choice in Nigeria, 10% of the respondents opined that they are not free to practice any religion in Nigeria, 4.6% of the respondents stated that they are not free at all to practice any religion in Nigeria, while 29.4% of the respondents are of the opinion that they are very free to practice any religion of their choice in Nigeria. This shows that the majority of the respondents in Nigeria are free to practice any religion of their choice in Nigeria. However, this could only be relative to Southern Nigeria because Christians in Northern Nigeria especially in North-Eastern Nigeria do not freely practice Christianity due to the fear of Boko Haram terrorists.

Table 20: Respondents' opinions on whether law enforcement agencies in Nigeria do not respect the rights of citizens

Law enforcement agencies do not respect the rights of their citizens.		
Responses	**Frequency**	**Percentages**
Strongly agree	129	62.3%
Agree	65	31.4%
Neither agree nor disagree	10	4.8%
Disagree	3	1.4%
Total	**207**	**100%**

Source: field survey, 2020.

Table 20 presents respondents' opinions on whether law enforcement agencies in Nigeria do not respect the rights of citizens. The result shows that 62.3% of the respondents strongly agreed that law enforcement agents in Nigeria do not respect the rights of their citizens, 31.4% of the respondents agreed that the law enforcement agencies in Nigeria do not respect the rights of citizens, 4.8% of the respondents neither agree nor disagree on whether law enforcement agencies respect the rights of the citizens, while 1.4% disagreed that law enforcement in their country does not respect their rights of the citizens. This implies that law enforcement agents in Nigeria do not respect the rights of the citizens. This could account for the high rate of brutality; extortion; intimidation; harassment; arbitrary arrest; illegal and elongated detention of innocent citizens by law enforcement agents in Nigeria.

Figure 19: Respondents' opinions on whether reinforcing the rights of women and girl child is very critical for sustainable development in Nigeria

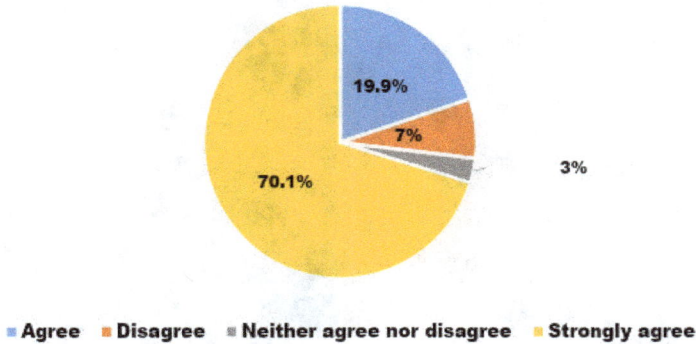

Source: field survey, 2020

Figure 19 presents respondents' opinions on whether reinforcing the rights of women and girl child is very critical for sustainable development in Nigeria. The result shows that 19.9% of the respondents agree that reinforcing the rights of women and girl child is very critical for sustainable development in Nigeria, 7% of the respondents disagreed, 5.6% of the respondents neither agree nor disagreed, while 70.1% of the respondents strongly agreed that reinforcing the rights of women and girl child is very critical for sustainable development in Nigeria. This shows that the majority (70.1%) of the respondents strongly agreed that reinforcing the rights of women and girl child is very critical for sustainable development in Nigeria. The above finding could be a result of the high level of marginalisation and exploitation of women and girl child in Nigeria.

Figure 20: Respondents' opinion on whether COVID-19 state response measures worsened the abuse of human rights in Nigeria

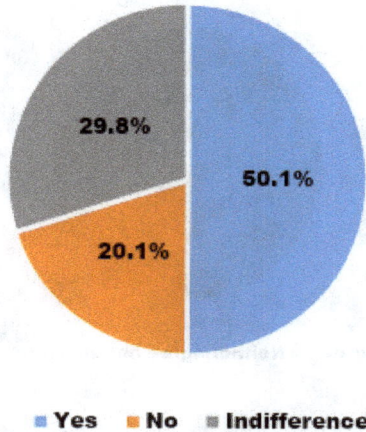

Source: field survey, 2020

Figure 20 is a pie chart showing respondents' opinions on whether Covid-19 and the state measures worsened the abuse of human rights in Nigeria. The result shows that 50.1% of the respondents said yes, that Covid-19 and the state measures worsened the abuse of human rights in Nigeria, 20.1% of the respondents said no, and that Covid-19 and the state measures did not worsen the abuse of human rights in Nigeria, while 29.4% of the respondents were indifferent on whether Covid-19 and the state measures worsened the abuse of human rights in Nigeria. This is an indication that Covid-19 and the state measures worsened the abuse of human rights in Nigeria. This finding could be buttressed by the fact that some people lost their lives not due to the Covid-19 pandemic but due to law enforcement brutalities, and extra-judicial killings during the Covid-19 lockdown.

Table 21: Respondents' opinions on ways their rights were abused

Brazen extortion by law enforcement of motorists and illegal and improper apprehension of people by law enforcement agents
Abuse by security forces during enforcement of mask usage/lockdown
Abuse of freedom by rights to worship and movement
Arbitrary arrest and detention
Attack by security agents on those who go out to seek food for their
Brutalisation by security agents
Closure of people's business without provision/alternative means of livelihood
Extorting money from civilians who didn't wear face masks and no provision was made for face mask
Abuse of rights of freedom of movement/association
Improper covid-19 protocol enforcements
Impunity by security agents enforcing lockdown rules
Increase in extortion and marginalisation of individuals on a daily basis
It increased injustice by security agents
Defaulters who didn't wear face masks or who moved out were flogged, tortured, and sometimes killed in the process
Restriction of my movement during the lockdown, unlawful arrest
Increase in rape cases and police violations

Source: field survey, 2020

Table 21 above presents respondents' opinion on ways Covid-19 worsen the abuse of human rights in Nigeria. The responses show that law enforcement brutality, violation and abuse of human rights, extortion, illegal detention, arbitrary arrest, torture of innocent citizens all in the name of enforcement of Covid-19 protocols. Restriction of movement during the lockdown and abuse of freedom of rights to worship are the ways the Covid-19 worsened the abuse of human rights in Nigeria.

Section E: Humanitarian Pillar

This section dealt with humanitarian pillars, respondents were asked to rate the effectiveness of humanitarianism in Nigeria, whether the humanitarian organisations in Nigeria have the capacity and flexibility to adjust and adapt and work in synergy with other stakeholders, roles civil societies organisation play in humanitarian and development works in Nigeria amongst other relevant questions were asked to the respondents and their responses and opinions are presented in tables and charts below.

Table 22: Respondents' ratings on the effectiveness of humanitarianism in Nigeria

How do you rate the effectiveness of humanitarianism in Nigeria?		
Ratings	**Frequency**	**Percentages**
Very effective	9	4.3%
Effective	78	37.7%
Ineffective	120	58%
Total	**207**	**100%**

Source: field survey, 2020

Table 22 presents respondents' ratings on the effectiveness of humanitarian interventions in Nigeria, the result shows that 4.3% of the respondents rated the effectiveness of humanitarianism in their country as very effective, 37.7% of the respondents rated the humanitarianism in Nigeria as effective, while 58% of the respondents opined that the humanitarianism in Nigeria is not effective. This implies that the majority (58%) of the respondents opined that humanitarianism was ineffective.

Figure 23: Respondents' opinions on what risk is more prevalent in Nigeria.

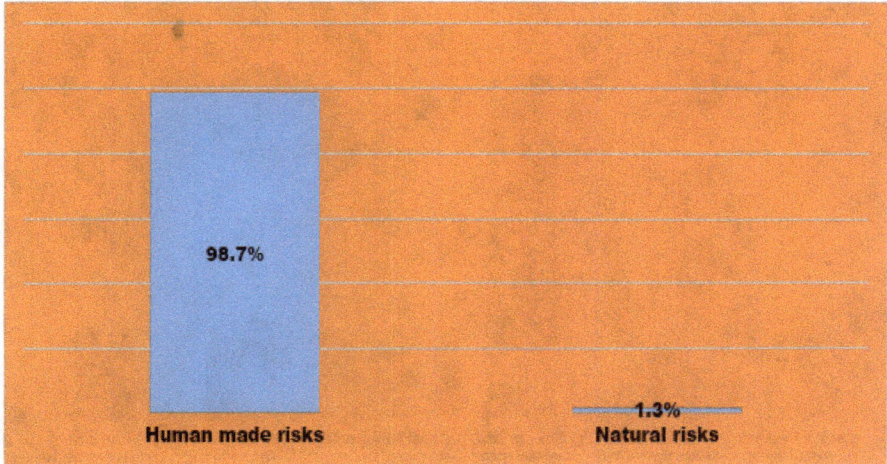

Source: field survey, 2020

Figure 23 presents respondents' opinions on what risk is more prevalent in Nigeria, the result shows that 98.7% of the respondents were of the opinion that human-made risks are more prevalent in Nigeria, while 1.3% of the respondents opined that natural risks are more prevalent in Nigeria. This is an indication that human-made risks are more prevalent in Nigeria. This is because issues of terrorism, kidnapping, and hostage-taking, armed robbery, violent conflicts, herders-farmers conflicts which lead to the displacement of some people are all human-made risks.

Figure 24: Respondents' opinions on the threats to the humanitarian pillar in Nigeria.

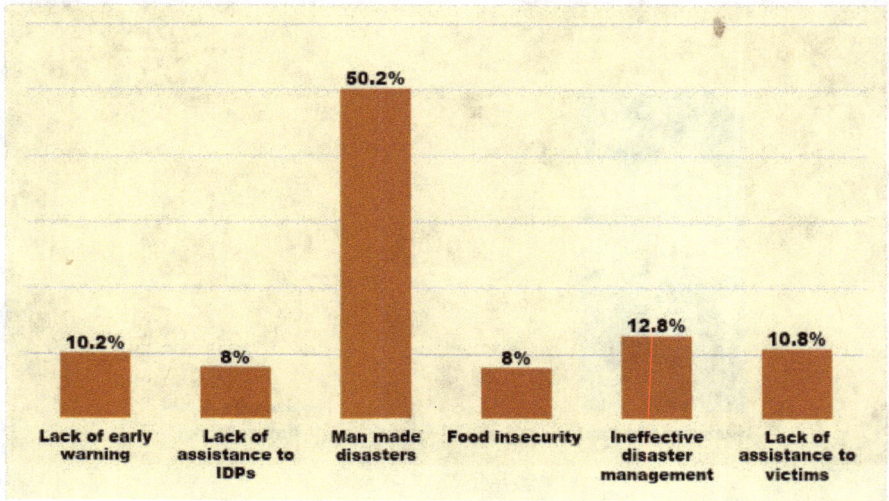

Source: field survey, 2020

Figure 24 presents respondents' opinions on the threats to the humanitarian pillar in Nigeria. The result shows that 10.2% of the respondents opined that lack of early earning is the major threat to the humanitarian pillar in their country, 8% of the respondents opined that lack of assistance to IDPs is the major threat to the humanitarian pillar, 50.2% of the respondents opined that manmade disasters are the major threats to humanitarian pillars in Nigeria 8% of the respondents stated that food insecurity is one of the major threats to humanitarian pillars in Nigeria, 12.8% of the respondents were of the opinion that ineffective disaster management is the major threat to humanitarian pillars in their community/country. While 10.8% of the respondents stated that lack of assistance to victims is a threat to the humanitarian pillar in Nigeria. This implies that man-made disasters are the major threat to the humanitarian pillar in Nigeria. The findings could be buttressed by the fact that man-made disasters like terrorism, banditry, kidnapping for ransom are threats to humanitarianism. For instance, some humanitarian workers were killed in Nigeria by the Boko Haram terrorists in 2019. This could deter other humanitarian workers from going to the North East of Nigeria for humanitarian work.

Figure 25: Respondents' opinions on whether humanitarian organisations in Nigeria have the capacity and flexibility to adjust and adapt and work in synergy with other stakeholders.

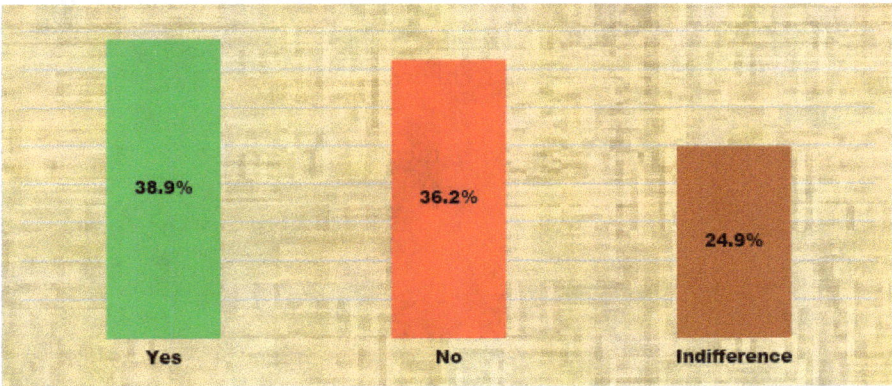

Source: field survey, 2020

Figure 25 presents respondents' opinions on whether humanitarian organisations in Nigeria have the capacity and flexibility to adjust and adapt and work in synergy with other stakeholders. The result shows that 38.9% of the respondents said yes; that humanitarian organisations in Nigeria have the capacity and flexibility to adjust and adapt and work in synergy with other stakeholders, 36.2% of the respondents said no that humanitarian organisations in Nigeria have the capacity and flexibility to adjust and adapt and work in synergy with other stakeholders, while 24.9% of the respondents were indifferent on whether humanitarian organisations in Nigeria have the capacity and flexibility to adjust and adapt and work in synergy with other stakeholders.

Table 23: Respondents' opinions on the most unmet humanitarian needs of your country

Most Unmet Humanitarian needs	Frequency	Percentage
Economic empowerment/Unemployment	37	17.9%
Youth empowerment	13	6.3%
Access to water and healthcare	9	4.3%
The needs of IDPs and street children/ Vulnerable population	16	7.7%
Beggars and persons living with mental illness	5	2.4%
Education	18	8.7%
Food	7	3.4%
Security	69	33.3%
Health	8	3.9%
Shelter	6	2.9%
Poverty	17	8.2%
Social welfare for the elder	2	1%
Total	**207**	**100%**

Source: field survey, 2020

Table 23 presents respondents' opinions on the most unmet humanitarian needs of Nigerians. The data shows that 17.9% of the respondents opined that economic empowerment/unemployment is the most unmet humanitarian need of Nigeria, 6.3% of the respondents said that youth empowerment is the most unmet need in Nigeria, 4.3% of the respondents said that access to water and health care is the most unmet humanitarian need in Nigeria, 7.7% of the respondents said that the needs of IDPs and street children/vulnerable population is the most unmet need in Nigeria, 2.4% of the respondents were of the opinion that beggars and person living with mental illness are the most unmet humanitarian needs in Nigeria, 8.7% of the respondents stated that education is the most unmet humanitarian needs in Nigeria. Also, 3.4% of the respondents said that food is the most unmet need in Nigeria, 33.3% of the respondents opined that security is the most unmet need in Nigeria, 3.9% of the respondents said that health is the most unmet humanitarian need in Nigeria, 2.9% of the respondents said that shelter is the most unmet humanitarian need in Nigeria, 8.2% of the respondents said that poverty is the most unmet humanitarian need in Nigeria, while 1% of the respondents opined that social welfare for the elder is the most unmet humanitarian need of their country. This is an indication that a higher percentage of the respondents is of the opinion that security is the most unmet humanitarian need of their country, followed by economic empowerment and unemployment.

Table 24: Respondents' opinions on the assertion that "humanitarian aids and support do not get to the people who need it in Nigeria"

Humanitarian aids and support do not get to the people who need it in your country.		
Response	**Frequency**	**Percentages**
Strongly agree	61	29.5%
Agree	129	62.3%
Neither agree nor disagree	10	4.8%
Disagree	7	3.4%
Total	**207**	**100%**

Source: field survey, 2020

Table 24 presents respondents' opinions on whether humanitarian aid and support do not get to the people who need it in Nigeria. The result shows that 29.5% of the respondents strongly agreed that humanitarian aids and support do not get to the people who need it in Nigeria, 62.3% of the respondents agreed that humanitarian aids and support do not get to the people who need it in Nigeria, 4.8% of the respondents neither agree nor disagreed that humanitarian aids and support do not get to the people who it in Nigeria, while 3.4% of the respondents disagreed that humanitarian aids and support do not get to the people who need it in Nigeria, this is an indication that humanitarian aids and support do not get to the people who need it in Nigeria.

Table 25: Respondents' opinions on the claim that "lack of good governance negatively affects humanitarian services in Nigeria"

Lack of good governance negatively affects humanitarian services in Nigeria?		
Opinion	**Frequency**	**Percentages**
Strongly agree	159	76.8
Agree	36	17.4
Neither agree nor disagree	12	5.8
Total	**207**	**100**

Source: field survey, 2020

Table 25 presents respondents' opinions on the claim that "lack of good governance negatively affects humanitarian services in Nigeria. The result shows that 76.8% of the respondents strongly agreed that lack of good governance negatively affects humanitarian services in Nigeria, 17.4% of the respondents agreed that lack of good governance negatively affects humanitarian services in their country, 5.8% of the respondents opined neither agreed nor disagreed that lack of good governance negatively affects humanitarian services in Nigeria. This shows that the lack of good governance negatively affects humanitarian services in Nigeria.

Table 26: Respondents' opinions on "targeting youth and women being critical in humanitarian services"

Targeting youth and women are critical in humanitarian services?		
Opinion	Frequency	Percentages
Strongly agree	162	78.3
Agree	33	15.9
Neither agree nor disagree	8	3.9
Disagree	4	1.9
Total	207	100%

Source: field survey, 2020

Table 26 presents respondents' opinions on whether targeting youth and women are critical in humanitarian service, the result shows that 78.3% of the respondents strongly agreed that targeting youths and women are critical in humanitarian services, 15.9% of the respondents agreed, 3.9% of the respondents neither agreed nor disagreed, while 1.9% of the respondents disagreed that targeting youth and women are critical in humanitarian services. This implies that targeting youth and women is critical in humanitarian services.

Figure 25: Respondents' opinions on whether "lack of neutrality" negatively affects humanitarian services

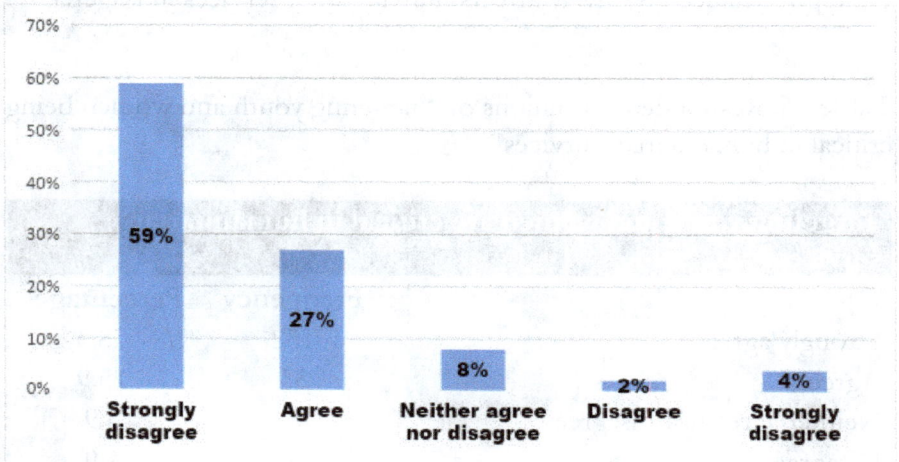

Source: field survey, 2020

Figure 25 presents respondents' opinions on whether lack of neutrality negatively affects humanitarian services. The result shows that 59% of the respondents strongly agreed that lack of neutrality negatively affects humanitarian services, 27% of the respondents agreed that lack of neutrality negatively affects humanitarian services, 8% of the respondents neither agree nor disagree that lack of neutrality negatively affects humanitarian services, 2% of the respondents disagreed that lack of neutrality negatively affects humanitarian services, while 4% of the respondents strongly disagreed that lack of neutrality negatively affects humanitarian services. This is an indication that a lack of neutrality negatively affects humanitarian services.

Section F: Interlinkage between the four pillars.

This section deals with the interlinkages among the four pillars. Respondents' opinions and responses are presented in the tables and charts below.

Table 27: Respondents' opinions on whether there is an interlink among peace and security, development, human rights, and humanitarian

There is an interlinkage among peace and security, development, human rights, and humanitarianism.		
Responses	**Frequency**	**Percentages**
Strongly agree	138	66.7%
Agree	46	22.2%
Neither agree nor disagree	23	11.1%
Total	**207**	**100%**

Source: field survey, 2020

Table 27 presents responses on whether there is an interlinkage among peace and security, development, human rights, and humanitarianism, the result shows that 66.7% of the respondents strongly agreed that there is an interlinkage between peace and security, development, human rights, and humanitarianism, 22.2% of the respondents agreed that there is an interlinkage among peace and security, development, human rights and humanitarianism, 11.1% of the respondents neither agree nor disagree that there are interlinkages. This shows that there is an interlinkage between peace and security, development, human rights, and humanitarianism.

Figure 26: Respondents' opinions on whether humanitarian and development actors work together in Nigeria.

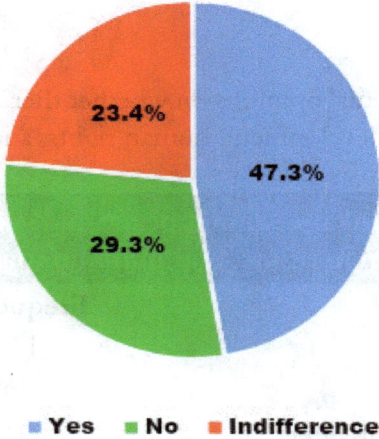

■ **Yes** ■ **No** ■ **Indifference**

Source: field survey, 2020

Figure 26 presents respondents' opinions on whether humanitarian and development actors work together in Nigeria, the result shows that 47.3% of the respondents said yes, that humanitarian and development actors work together in Nigeria, 29.3% of the respondents said no that humanitarian and development actors do not work together in Nigeria, while 23.4% of the respondents were indifferent to the assertion that humanitarian and development actors work together in Nigeria. This is an indication that humanitarian and development actors work together in Nigeria.

Table 28: Respondents' opinions on ways human rights complement peace and security in Nigeria

Proper knowledge about human rights and how not to trample on the rights of others is important for peace and security
By allowing the freedom of association which is essential to development, peace, and security
Ensuring respect to lives and property will enhance peace, security, and development
Freedom of speech creates room for dialogue during conflict and freedom of worship makes most people better human
Human rights bring about freedom and justice. This naturally breeds peace, security, and development
Human rights complement peace and security when it is upheld and it gives hope to people who are being marginalised
Human rights contribute to justice and that is linked to peace and security
Human rights ensure effective synergy between peace, security, and development
Human rights encourage one to work with confidence and optimally and that enhances the development
The promotion of human rights will promote peace, security, and development
When the human rights of citizens are respected especially by the government and law enforcement agencies it brings about the development

Source: field survey, 2020

Table 28 presents respondents' opinions on ways human rights complement peace and security and development. The result shows that a high level of human rights will lead to development in many ways, e.g., a proper knowledge about human rights and how not to trample on the rights of others is important for peace and security; freedom of speech creates room for dialogue during conflict and freedom of worship makes most people better human. Moreover, human rights encourage one to work with confidence and optimality and that enhances development.

Table 29: Respondents' opinion on whether lack of peace and security hinders development

Lack of peace and security hinders development?		
Responses	**Frequency**	**Percentages**
Strongly agree	189	91.3%
Agree	16	7.7%
Disagree	2	1%
Total	**207**	**100%**

Source: field survey, 2020

Table 29 presents respondents' opinions on whether lack of peace and security hinders development. The result shows that 91.3% of the respondents strongly agreed that lack of peace and security hinders development, 7.7% of the respondents agreed that lack of peace and security hinders development, 1% of the respondents disagreed that lack of peace and security hinders development. This is an indication that lack of peace and security hinders development in Nigeria.

Table 30: Respondents' opinions on whether underdevelopment is the cause and effect of human rights abuse in Nigeria

Underdevelopment is the cause and effect of human rights abuse in your country.		
Responses	**Frequency**	**Percentages**
Strongly agree	134	64.7%
Agree	60	29%
Neither agree nor disagree	4	1.9%
Disagree	3	1.4%
Strongly disagree	6	2.9%
Total	**207**	**100%**

Source: field survey, 2020

Table 30 presents respondents' opinions on whether underdevelopment is the cause and effect of human rights abuse in Nigeria, the result shows that 64.7% of the respondents strongly agreed that underdevelopment is the cause and effect of human rights abuse in Nigeria, 29% agreed to the above assertion, 1.9% of neither agree nor disagree with the above assertion, 1.4% of the respondents disagreed to the above assertion, while 2.9% of the respondents strongly disagreed that underdevelopment is the cause and effect of human right abuse in Nigeria. This is an indication that underdevelopment is the cause and effect of human rights abuse in Nigeria.

Table 31: Respondents' opinions on whether human rights violation is the major cause of conflict in Nigeria

Human rights violation is the major cause of conflict in Nigeria?		
Ratings	Frequency	Percentages
Yes	147	71
No	38	18.4
Indifference	22	10.6
Total	**207**	**100**

Source: field survey, 2020

Table 31 presents respondents' opinions on whether human rights violation is the major cause of conflict in Nigeria, the result shows that 71% of the respondents said yes, that human rights violation is the major cause of conflict in Nigeria. 18.4% of the respondents said no, that human rights violations are not the major cause of conflict in Nigeria, 10.6% of the respondents were indifferent to the assertion that human rights violation is the major cause of conflict in Nigeria. This is an indication that human rights violation is the major cause of conflict in Nigeria.

Figure 27: Respondents' opinions on whether there have been opportunities in the application of the interlinkages approach for conflict prevention and resolution

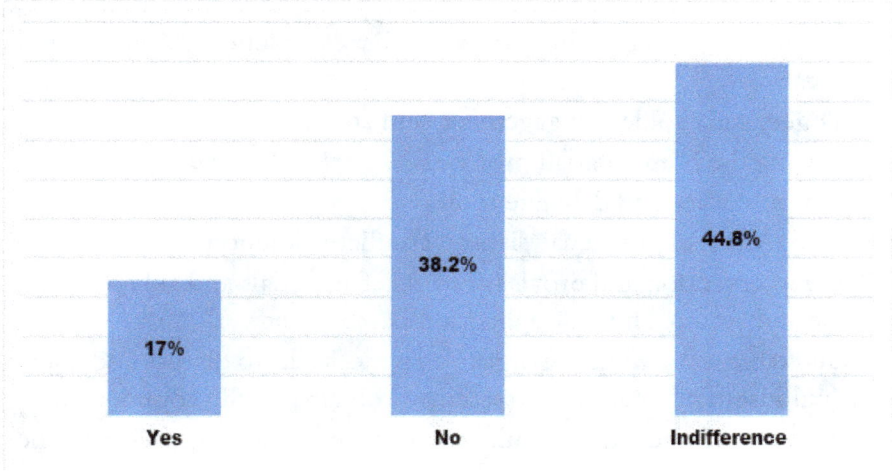

Source: field survey, 2020

Figure 27 presents respondents' opinions on whether there have been opportunities in the application of the inter-linkages approach for conflict prevention and resolution. The result shows that 17% of the respondents said yes, that there have been opportunities in the application of the inter-linkages approaches for conflict prevention and resolution, 38.2% of the respondents said no that there have been no opportunities in the application of the inter-linkages approaches for conflict prevention and resolution, while 44.8% of the respondents were indifference to the assertion that there have been opportunities in the application of the inter-linkages approach for conflict prevention and resolution.

Table 32: Respondents' opinions on whether their institutions or organisations have been utilizing methodologies and tools for integrating the four pillars into policies and practices

Community peacebuilding and conflict resolution training and advocacy
Dialogue, stakeholders engagement, and advocacy
Following the humanitarian protocols
We use advocacy and dialogue tools
Peacebuilding, conflict analysis, and conflict resolution
Policy intervention and provision of relief materials and aid to ensure, peace and security, human rights, and development
Round table workshops are organised periodically to discuss and come up with useful resolutions to teething problems of the community.
Being part of the early warning system and fostering policy in the public and private sectors on gender and social inclusion

Source: field survey, 2020

Table 32 presents respondents' opinions on methodologies and tools their institutions or organisations have been using for integrating the four pillars into policies and practices. The result shows that some of the respondents opined that the methodology they use is community peacebuilding, conflict resolution training, and advocacy; dialogue and stakeholders engagement and advocacy; Policy intervention, provision of relief materials and aids; being part of the early warning system and fostering policy in the public and private sectors on gender and social inclusion.

Figure 28: Respondents' opinions on opportunities in the application of the interlinkages approach for conflict prevention and resolution

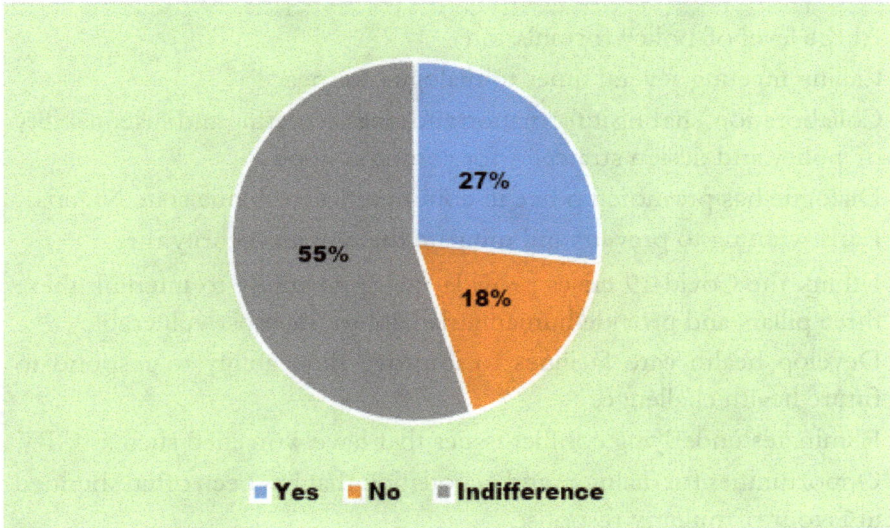

Source: field survey, 2020

Figure 28 is a pie chart showing respondents' opinions on the opportunities in the application of the interlinkages approach for conflict prevention and resolution, the result shows that 27% of the respondents said yes, that there are opportunities in the application of the interlinkages approach for conflict prevention and resolution, 18% said no, while 55% of the respondents were indifference on whether there are opportunities in the application of the interlinkages approach for conflict prevention and resolution.

Table 33: Respondents' opinions opportunities in the application of the interlinkages approach for conflict prevention and resolution in Nigeria

At the level of policy formulation
Calling meeting several times to dialogue for peace
Collaboration, sharing information and ideas, fostering and sustainability of policy and design strategies for common good
Dialogue has promoted peace in communities in Benue state Nigeria
Early warning to prevent and mitigate the human security threat
I think the Covid-19 crises provide the opportunity to interlink these three pillars and provide humanitarian aid to the most vulnerable
Develop health care facilities to improve their ability to respond to future health challenges
Eliminates underlying conflict issues that have worsened such as GBV
Opportunities for dialogue and negotiation that has been often shunned in favour of military response
Collaboration with government agencies
Policy dialogues

Source: field survey, 2020

Table 33 shows opportunities in the application of the interlinkages approach for conflict prevention and resolution, which includes calling meeting several times to dialogue for peace, collaboration, sharing information and ideas, fostering and sustainability of policy and design strategies for common good, dialogues has promoted peace in communities, elimination of underlying conflict issues that worsened amongst other opportunities.

Figure 29: Respondents' opinions on whether there have been challenges in the application of the interlinkages approach for conflict prevention and resolution

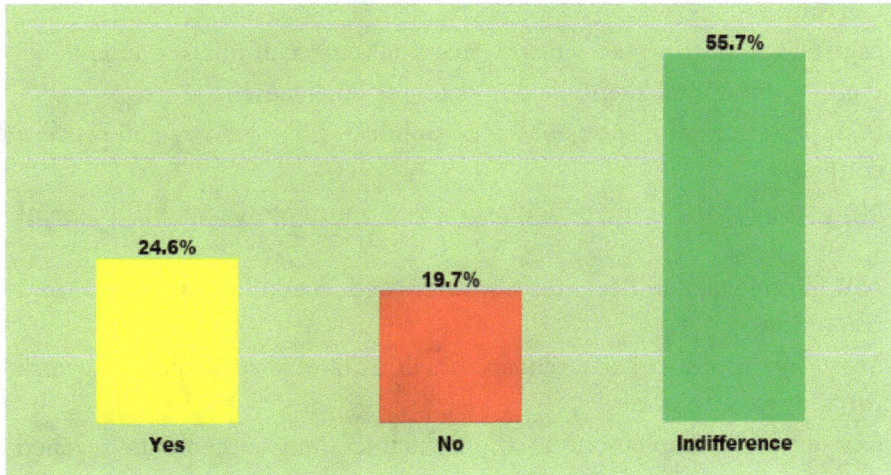

Source: field survey, 2020

Figure 29 presents respondents' opinions on whether there have been challenges in the application of the interlinkages approach for conflict prevention and resolution. The result shows that 24.6% of the respondents said yes, that there have been challenges in the application of the interlinkages approach for conflict prevention and resolution, 19.7% of the respondents said no that there have been no challenges in the application of the interlinkages approaches for conflict prevention and resolution, 55.7% of the respondents were indifferent to the assertion that there been challenges in the application of the inter-linkages approach for the conflict prevention and resolution. This shows that there have been challenges in the application of the interlinkages approach for conflict prevention and resolution in Nigeria.

Table 34: Challenges in the application of the interlinkages approaches for conflict prevention and resolution in Nigeria

Corruption
Injustice, nepotism, favouritism, marginalisation, ethnic sentiments
Getting the right stakeholders in dialogue engagement
Poor government response/lack of political will to resolve and prevent conflicts
Non respect for human rights by state actors and law enforcement agents
Not all the stakeholders are fully interested in conflict prevention and resolution
Most organisation in different sectors don't have a workable framework for conflict resolution
Resistance to implementing the principles and agreements reached during dialogues

Source: field survey, 2020

Table 34 presents challenges in the application of the interlinkages approach for conflict prevention and resolution. The result shows that corruption; injustice, nepotism, favouritism, marginalisation and, ethnic sentiments are some of the challenges in the application of the interlinkages approach for conflict prevention and resolution. Moreover, poor government responses and lack of political will to resolve and prevent conflicts is also another challenge in the application of the interlinkages approach for conflict prevention and resolution. Others include lack of trust and understanding, non-respect for human rights by state actors, and bad governance; terrorism, not all stakeholders are fully interested in conflict resolution and prevention. Other challenges include the fact that most organisations in different sectors do not have a workable framework for conflict resolution, resistance to implementing the principles and agreements reached during dialogues.

Table 35: Respondents' opinions on how the four pillars could be harnessed or promote complementary interventions to contribute to the effective lasting resolution to conflicts

Good governance will help promote effective lasting solutions to conflicts
The four (4) pillars should have research and development units to provide second inputs to policies in a constantly evolving political-economic and socio-cultural environment
Transparency in all aspects will help contribute to an effective lasting solutions to conflicts
The four pillars are institutionally weak, they will require adequate financial and human resources for robust operations to achieve set objectives
All stakeholders in the four pillars must work to contribute to effective lasting solutions to conflict only when corrupt practices, nepotism, and favouritism have been curbed to the barest minimum
Both the public and private sectors should synergize in sincerity and truth
By effectively collaborating with the relevant stakeholder from state and non-state actors
By ensuring that principles of humanitarian are strictly adhered to
Consultation, sensitisation, training, and participation in decision making
Education of youths on these four pillars will be fundamental in effective lasting solutions to conflicts
Equity and fairness
The four pillars will complement each other when the practitioners focus on synergizing through the humanitarian-development and peacebuilding (HDP) nexus.
Through effective implementation of policies
When peace is allowed by respecting human rights

Source: field survey, 2020

Table 35 shows respondents' comments on how the four pillars could be harnessed to contribute to effective lasting solutions to conflicts. The result shows that good governance will help promote effective lasting solutions to conflict. Transparency in all aspects will help contribute to effective lasting solutions to conflict. Moreover, all stakeholders in the four pillars must work in synergy to ensure peace and security. In the same vein, both the public and private sectors must work in synergy in sincerity and truth to contribute to effective lasting solutions to conflicts. The four pillars should have research and development units to provide some inputs to policies in a constantly evolving political, economic, and socio-cultural environment.

Chapter Four

Concluding Remarks

The reactions of Nigerians through the survey shows exasperation on insecurity in the country. Nigeria has not performed well on the most sacred reason for coming together as a nation-state. The consequences are the spate of kidnappings of school children and adults alike for ransom; terrorist attacks from within and from outside Nigeria's borders; wanton destruction of lives and livelihoods in the herders/farmers conflicts.

A cursory look at some key development indicators in the last ten years reflects the generally weak position of the Nigerian state. Nigeria's performance on the SDGs overall ranking has been dismal. In 2020, Nigeria ranked 160th out of 193 countries.[1] In the following year 2021, data was only available for 165 countries and Nigeria kept its miserable position of 160th.[2] In the Corruption Perception Index ratings by Transparency International, Nigeria in the last ten years out of about 170-180 countries, has appeared within the range of 134th-144th position, scoring between 24-27 out of 100[3]. In the 2021 CPI figures from Tansparency International, Nigeria worsened by scoring 24 out

---

1 https://sustainabledevelopment.un.org/memberstates/nigeria
2 https://dashboards.sdgindex.org/rankings
3 Cumulative CPI ranking published annually.

of 100 and ranking 154th out of 180 countries. This is a drop of five places in comparison with the previous position of 149[4]. In the UNDP Human Development Index, which cumulatively measures progress on longevity and healthy life, access to knowledge, standard of living and gross national income per capita, Nigeria has ranked between 156-157 out of 189 countries over a consecutive period of time.[5] Looking at the Happiness Index that measures about 156 countries, Nigeria has ranked between 78-103 in the recent periods[6] On the issue of Press Freedom Index, from 180 countries accessed annually, Nigeria has ranked between 111-135 over a long stretch of time.[7] On the Ease of Doing Business, from a total of 190 countries, Nigeria has ranked between 131-170 in the last decade. Data from the World Bank shows that in 2018 alone, 40% of Nigerians amounting to 83 million, lived below the poverty line. This is projected to rise by 12 million between 2019-2023. Another 25%, about 53 million people, are being described as vulnerable.[8] The 2020 Human Capital Index of the World Bank ranked Nigeria as 150 of 157 countries.

Nigerian youths, fed up with abuses and harassments resorted to a social unrest and mass protest against police brutality in the country calling for disbanding of the Special Anti-Robbery Squad (SARS), a notorious unit of the police force with a long record of abuses, corruption, unlawful arrests, detention and extrajudicial killings. The mass demonstrations occurred in much of Nigeria. The #EndSARS protest started between the 8th of October 2020.[9] The Lagos protest took a different dimension with the military deployed to the Lekki Toll Gate, the epicenter of

---

4 See, Punch and Guardian newspapers of January 25, 2022 among others. It is needless to repeat that, the survey in this study supports Transparency Internationals, in spite of fault finding efforts of Nigeria government officials.

5 UNDP HDI reports

6 World happiness reports

7 The Human Freedom Index

8 The World Bank in Nigeria

9 Lagos State Judicial Panel of Inquiry on Restitution for Victims of SARS related Abuses and other Matters. Report of Lekki Incident Investigation of 20th October 2020.

the protest in Lagos, on the night of October 20, 2020.[10] The Judicial Panel set up by Babajide Sanwo-Olu, the Governor of Lagos State, to undertake an inquiry into what happened stated as follows: "From all available evidence, it is without doubt that the military did not just use blank ammunition at Lekki Toll Gate. The eyewitness accounts show very clearly that live ammunition was used by the military, who were initially the only persons who carried arms to the protest ground on the day of the incident. The medical evidence on the nature of the injury sustained by the protesters and cases of death were results of the deployment of live ammunition as confirmed by the forensic experts, Sentinel Forensic Limited and Oxygen consulting UK Limited"[11]

The insurgency in the Northeast by the militant terrorist groups Boko Haram and the Islamic State West Africa Province, are major human rights threats. The groups conducted numerous attacks on government and civilian targets, resulting in thousands of deaths and injuries, widespread destruction and internal displacements.

At the humanitarian level, the picture is not salutary. Nigeria, as at October 31, 2021, was having 3,033,363 internally displaced persons with most resulting from conflicts.[12] Aside from conflict and insecurity, the Food and Agriculture Organisation (FAO) notes that climate change and degradation of natural resources are also worsening the humanitarian situation in Nigeria. This situation has been confounded by the COVID-19 pandemic.[13]

There are a number of areas where the Nigerian economy reflects some appreciable levels of development, especially on a comparative scale with the overall performance of the country, if not at the global level. The

---

10 Ibid.

11 Ibid., 289

12 https://data2.unhcr.org/en/country/nga

13 FAO, The Federal Republic of Nigeria Resilience Strategy 2021–2023 Increasing the resilience of agriculture-based livelihood: The pathway to humanitarian–development–peace nexus, 2021.

Nigerian entertainment industry, comprising the film, music, comedy, writing and all kinds of creativities as sub industries have commanded some global leading growth. For example, Nigeria produces around 2,500 films yearly, an amazing figure that makes it the second biggest global film production hub behind India.[14] There is the potential for soft-power for Nigeria in this area if harnessed.

Nigerian tech startups are pulling some punches on the African continent with the top 10 comprising almost exclusively of Nigerian startups Africa[15]. According to Bloomberg, in October 2021, Flutterwave was in talks to triple its valuation to $3 Billion.[16] Paystack, providing modern online and offline payments services for users across the continent was acquired by Stripe in 2020 for over $200 million in what was one of the biggest exits in the African tech space.[17]

Nonetheless, the situation is overall not looking good. The survey of 207 informed Nigerians support approaching the amelioration of the problem using a situational quadruple nexus analysis. There are strong interlinkages or put another way, nexuses between the four pillars for the analysis, and/or operational efforts towards the good life in Nigeria, nay Africa, if not humanity. These pillars are peace/security; development; human rights and humanitarian affairs. The quadruple nexus or four-pillar interlinkages offer the opportunity for a comprehensive understanding of the situations in national, regional, or international organisations. For operational responses in having coherent and synergistic as well as efficient efforts on pushing nations, regions and, humanity towards the good life or utmost freedom on earth, the quadruple nexus also known as four-pillar interlinkages come in very handy.

---

14 Pwc report, The Business of Entertainment, Harnessing growth opportunities in entertainment, media, arts and lifestyle.

15 Ejike Kanife, Nigerian tech startups are building the most exciting brands in Africa as they dominate top 20 Challenger brands. Technext.

16 Gillian Tan, Nigeria's Flutterwave in Talks to Triple Valuation to $3 Billion. Bloomberg. October 14, 2021.

17 Ejike Kanife, *op. cit.*

However, this study supports the strong position that the quadruple nexus or four-pillar interlinkages are not enough for either analysis or operational efforts. Four situational foundations that serve as an environment for the quadruple nexus must also be in clear focus. These four situational foundations include governance, external dynamics, institutions, and resources. When both quadruple realities are coupled, we have situational quadruple nexus.

Situational quadruple nexus as a framework is important in understanding the interconnectedness of the four main pillars towards the realisation of utmost freedom in any political society. More importantly, is the fact that the framework, unlike many others, strives for solutions to lack of peace, development, respect for human rights as well as inability to cope with humanitarian situations within overarching four fundamental issues of concern. These are governance (with major attention on leadership deficit and corruption), external dynamics (which is crucial for weak nations but normally wished away by "aid" workers), institutions, and resources.

It is impossible to engage in the realisation of improvements on the interconnectedness of the four pillars when there are fundamental problems with the situational foundation on which the pillars rest. Expectedly, these pillars will not implement themselves in a situation of deficits in governance and when the external dynamics are weighing down on the organised political society. Getting governance right could go some way in reducing the dangers at the level of external dynamics as well as ensure that the process of building institutions commence with available resources, however limited.

Utmost freedom is the optimal desire of human beings to have several freedoms to operate in a political society. The freedoms would also include freedom from hindrances to the good life. In effect, while utmost freedom is an ideal, efforts towards it can be conceptualised as the summation of all the freedoms inherent in the SDGs.

Oftentimes, and more so in Nigeria, policy interventions and actions are based on the views of a limited number of stakeholders, including "aid" workers who in turn are pushed by strong external actors as well as those in control of the state machinery. Oftentimes, little attention is paid to the views of the public at large. This study provides a clear picture of the views of Nigerians on the state of peace, and by implication development, human rights, and humanitarian affairs in Nigeria.

This study relied on the views of a representative number of informed Nigerians. The normal governmental brouhaha reactions on some of these issues, (especially when external actors award rankings to Nigeria on internationally aggregated lists) is avoided in this study. For example, in spite of the abundant evidence on the worsening situation in Nigeria with respect to corruption, including under the Buhari administration, the spokespersons of the administration have tended to always denounce the corruption perception index (CPI) of Transparency International for being inaccurate. In this study, Nigerians have overwhelmingly responded that corruption is not only rife but that the level of corruption has been having a negative impact on the four pillars and their interlinkages.

This study provides technical support and advice to achieving peace, development, respect for human rights as well as the building of resilience on humanitarian affairs in Nigeria.

Overall, Nigerians have responded on several issues that are useful in understanding why the country is facing conflicts, failure on development (in spite of claims on so much in resources being devoted to development), failure to realise respect for human rights in spite of accession to several instruments including the Nigerian Constitution that expects the Nigerian government to perform on human rights as well as the inability of the Nigerian government to build resilience to absorb natural and man-made humanitarian problems. Responses to humanitarian problems have also been inadequate as per the views of Nigerians. And this situation is in spite of the establishment of a Ministry of Humanitarian Affairs by the Buhari administration. The expected positive support to Nigerians in ameliorating the negative impact of Covid-19 has taken place, only on paper in spite of the claims of President Buhari during the 76th UN General Assembly.

The Buhari administration cannot come anywhere near the realisation of the SDGs that it signed on to in spite of claims to the contrary. The popular reaction of Nigerians in this study, is in accord with the fact that Nigeria has been dubbed the poverty capital of the world.

Finally, Nigeria has been declared independent since 1960. However, it is wrong to continue operating in the Eurocentric orientation as if there was no history of the country before colonisation. The geographical expression called Nigeria was not tabula rasa on October 1, 1960. Dynamic entities had offered comparable contemporaneous development examples that compared favourably with Europe. Without going back to the pyramids and hieroglyphics of Egypt and Sudan, the sophisticated developments and ideas in the Benin Kingdom and Oyo Empire are too glaring to be unnoticed. Despite some denial efforts, the looted artefacts as well as other records are clear enough to show that the people of Nigeria were on their path of cultured development and were making contributions to human civilisation already. But that was before the arms race resulted in the English invention of the Maxim gun that worked against the Ijebu and Bini people respectively. This resulted in colonial suzerainty over Southern Nigeria as others principalities capitulated without much resistance. However, the colonial hiatus, in spite of its debilitating plunder, should not have created an irreparable underdevelopment. Obafemi Awolowo in Western Nigeria achieved so much under self-government that surpassed some other competing civilisations.

Nigeria's problems rests on leadership deficit/corruption which are at the core of misgovernance. One can add the rule of law in spite of that being superfluous given the inverse relationship between corruption and the rule of law. However, the misgovernance problem must be examined along with the external dynamics. It is a competitive world in which no-one owes Nigeria, nay Africa, a living. It is in the interests of others to destabilise Nigeria and fan the embers that keep the country down.

This must be acknowledged as being a present problematic factor to be consciously addressed. This is not a blame game but an analysis of the international environment in which countries emphasise their interests as primary. It is for a visionary leadership to steer Nigeria away from obstacles to move as near as possible to utmost freedom or at least a salutary effort on achieving the SDGs.

Other relevant issues are modernising Nigerian institutions towards development as the country eschews imposed values and orientations, especially religious ones that aided its colonisation and continue to serve as an opium that tranquilises Nigeria away from utmost freedom. In addition, democratic values (when the emphasis is on electoral contests which in many parts of Africa are triggers for instability) is dysfunctional for development. Democracy seen as aiming for popularised optimal collective interests (favouring drastic reductions of injustices, inequalities and inequities), as opposed to individualised protection of greed, could be useful for the realisation of SDGs. On resources as the fourth area of focus towards utmost freedom, Nigeria is blessed with respect to human and material dimensions.

In sum, with a realisation that development is just one of four pillars for a progressive forward march, with the others being peace and security; respect for human rights and humanitarian resilience, it is possible to move ahead. But these interconnected pillars can only be properly harnessed once one addresses the earlier mentioned implementation foundations. These include addressing simultaneously, leadership deficit/corruption (which will take care of rule of law), debilitating and destabilising external dynamics, Nigeria's deficits in authentic and modernised institutions and of course optimal egalitarian deployment of human and material resources. It must constantly be realised that Nigeria exists in a competitive world in which others cannot but be covetous of the resources it has.

Utmost freedom is an ideal situation worth striving for. Paradise, in effect, can start on earth as opposed to waiting for it in the assumed idyllic state of heaven that is subscribed to by some religions. Striving for utmost freedom on earth would involve appreciable progress on the SDGs.

Nigeria is far from ensuring utmost freedom for its citizens. Situational quadruple nexus could help in moving forward on what can be done.

Annex

N.B. This is a replication of the Survey used in the ECA study from which the specificities on Nigeria were extracted.

Questionnaire on Peace and Security, Human Rights, Humanitarian, and Development.

Survey Questionnaire

> **Dear participant,**
>
> Please provide your opinion about the issues raised in the questionnaire, which would take about 10 to 15 minutes.
>
> The questionnaire is designed to be anonymous. Your response will be confidential. You have the right to refuse to answer any question – it is totally voluntary. Completion and return of this questionnaire imply consent to share towards knowledge on issues raised.

INSTRUCTIONS ON HOW TO COMPLETE THE SURVEY

1	2
Read each question carefully.	Answer each question by filling in the required space, and putting an ☒ or a ☑ in the box of your choice, unless asked otherwise.

SECTION A: Socio-demographic and general profile of respondents

This set of questions is about you

S/N	QUESTIONS	RESPONSES	CODE
A1	**Sex**		
		Male	1
		Female	2
		Others	3
A2	**Age**		
A3	**Marital status**		
		Married	1
		Single	2
		Divorced	3
		Separated	4
		Widowed	5
A4	**Highest education complemented**		
		No formal education	1
		Primary school	2
		Secondary school	3
		Tertiary education	4
		Post tertiary	5

A5a	Sector		
		Public (Government) Sector	1
		Non State	2
		Regional/International Institutions	3

A5b	Specific sector		
		Development	1
		Regional and International work	2
		NGO/Humanitarian work	3
		Private work	4
		Legal/Human rights	5
		Academic and Media	6

A6	Country		

A7	Region		
		Central Africa	1
		West Africa	2

A8	How prevalent are conflicts (simmering tensions, violent conflicts and protracted conflicts) in your country?		
		Highly prevalent	1
		Prevalent	2
		Not prevalent	3

A9	Can you mention the prevention and resolution approaches employed in your country to tackle these conflicts?	

Section B: Peace and Security

Please tick ☑ the correct answer and also fill in the appropriate response by giving the necessary details in the spaces provided below.

S/N	QUESTIONS	RESPONSES	CODE
B1a	How do you rate the peace and security situation in your country?		
		Low Peace and Security	1
		Medium Peace and security	2
B1b	How do you rate the peace and security situation in your subregion?		
		Low Peace and security	1
		Medium Peace and security	2
		High Peace and security	3
		Very High Peace and security	4
B2	What are the threats to peace and security in your country and subregion?		
		Tick as many that apply	
		Violent crimes	1
		Terrorism	2
		Electoral violence	3
		Herders-farmers conflict	4
		Religious extremism	5
		Maritime piracy	6
		Inequality/Injustice	7

Greed/Corruption/Mismanagement	8
Grievance	9
Inter/intra community conflict	10
Youth delinquency/violence	11
Climate change risks	12
Drug trafficking	13
Human trafficking	14
Separatism/Rebellion	15
Unemployment	16
Others specify	
_____	

B3   **Which peace and security threat is/are most prevalent in your community or country?**

B4   **What factors would you say promotes/encourages the threats to peace and security in your country?**

B5a   **Has the Covid-19 pandemic affected your safety and security?**

Yes	1
No	2
Indifference	3

B5b	If yes in B5a above, please specify in what way(s) the pandemic have affected your safety and security?

B6a	Is the fear of the police force and other security agents a major concern in your community or country?	
	Yes	1
	No	2
	Indifference	3

B6b	If yes in B6a above, please state why you are afraid of police and other security agents in your community or country?

B7	Does terrorism pose an immediate challenge to you and your household in your country?	
	Yes	1
	No	2
	Indifference	3

B8	Are corruption and lack of transparency the greatest threat to achieving peace and security?	
	Strongly agree	1
	Agree	2
	Neither agree nor disagree	3
	Disagree	4
	Strongly disagree	5

B9	In the past 12 months preceding this study, how many times have you or your household been a victim of insecurity? For example, robbed, attacked?	

B10	How often do people suffer loss of properties, assets or investment as a result of insecurity issues in your community/country?	
	Very often	1
	Often	2
	Not very often	3
	Rarely	4

B11	Does fear of crime and insecurity affect business activities in your community or country?	
	Yes	1
	No	2
	Indifference	3

B12	How much do you trust the state security system?	
	High trust	1
	Low trust	2
	Don't trust them at all	3

B13	A society where conflicts are resolved peacefully through dialogue would experience sustainable development faster?	
	Strongly agree	1
	Agree	2
	Neither agree nor disagree	3
	Disagree	4
	Strongly disagree	5

B14a	Religious intolerance is a major threat to peace and security in your country?	
	Yes	1
	No	2
	Indifference	3

B14b	If yes, please could you explain how?

B15	Does lack of good governance in your country hinder the existence of peace and security?	
	Strongly agree	1
	Agree	2
	Neither agree nor disagree	3
	Disagree	4
	Strongly disagree	5

B16	Do perceptions on ethnic marginalisation and such grievances account for violent conflicts in your country?	
	Yes	1
	No	2
	Indifference	3

B17	If yes, please elaborate how ethnic marginalisation and grievances have caused violent conflict and tension in your country?

Section C: Development

Please tick ☑ the correct answer and also fill in the appropriate response by giving the necessary details in the spaces provided.

S/N	QUESTIONS	RESPONSES	CODE
C1	How do you rate the level of development in your state and country?		
		Highly developed	1
		Adequately Developed	2
		Underdeveloped	3
C2	Which of the following do you think hinders development in your state and country?		
		Tick as many that apply	
		Bribery/corruption	1
		Bad/greedy leaders	2
		Violent crimes	3
		Lack of education	4
		Capital Flight	5
		Fragility of political institutions	6
		Inequality/Injustice	7
		Lack of social protection	8
		Greed	9
		Ethnic grievances	10
		Inter/intra community conflict	11
		Youth violence/gang	12
		Climate change risks	13

	Unemployment	14
	Lack of access to health care	15
	Lack of financial resources (SMEs)	16
	Others specify	
	_____	

C3   Are corruption and lack of transparency the greatest issues in development?

	Strongly agree	1
	Agree	2
	Neither agree nor disagree	3
	Disagree	4
	Strongly disagree	5

C4   Is freedom of democratic rights critical for sustainable development?

	Strongly agree	1
	Agree	2
	Neither agree nor disagree	3
	Disagree	4
	Strongly disagree	5

C5   Is respecting human rights the most critical issue in sustainable development?

	Strongly agree	1
	Agree	2
	Neither agree nor disagree	3
	Disagree	4
	Strongly disagree	5

C6a	Has ethnic marginalisation and economic deprivation retarded development in some part of your country?	
	Yes	1
	No	2
	Indifference	3

C6b	If yes, can you mention ethnic groups that are less developed in your country and why?

C7	Cultural/religious tolerance is critical for sustainable development?	
	Strongly agree	1
	Agree	2
	Neither agree nor disagree	3
	Disagree	4
	Strongly disagree	5

C8	Do poor people around you have access to education in your community and country?	
	Yes	1
	No	2
	Indifference	3

C9	How difficult is it for the poor to secure modest accommodation in your community?	
	Very easy	1
	Easy	2
	Difficult	3
	Very difficult	4

C10	Poor access to low quality infrastructure is a major threat to sustainable development?		
		Strongly agree	1
		Agree	2
		Neither agree nor disagree	3
		Disagree	4
		Strongly disagree	5

C11	Providing young people with access to quality education is a prerequisite for development?		
		Strongly agree	1
		Agree	2
		Neither agree nor disagree	3
		Disagree	4
		Strongly disagree	5

C12a	Has the Covid-19 pandemic affected your source of livelihood?		
		Yes	1
		No	2
		Indifference	3

C12b	If yes, to question C12a above, please can you state how it affected your source of livelihood?

C13   **Environmental preservation is critical for sustainable development?**

	Strongly agree	1
	Agree	2
	Neither agree nor disagree	3
	Disagree	4
	Strongly disagree	5

C14   **Empowering youth and women are critical for sustainable development?**

	Strongly agree	1
	Agree	2
	Neither agree nor disagree	3
	Disagree	4
	Strongly disagree	5

C15   **Improving healthcare is necessary for sustainable development?**

	Strongly agree	1
	Agree	2
	Neither agree nor disagree	3
	Disagree	4
	Strongly disagree	5

C16   **How can civil society organisations promote sustainable development in your state and country?**

135

Section D: Human Rights

Please tick ☑ the correct answer and also fill in the appropriate response by giving the necessary details in the spaces provided.

S/N	QUESTIONS	RESPONSES	CODE
D1	**How do you rate the level of respect for human rights in your country?**		
		Highly developed	1
		High	2
		Medium	3
		Low	4
		Very low	5

S/N	QUESTIONS	RESPONSES	CODE
D2	**What do you consider the greatest threat to human rights in your country?**		
		Tick all that apply	
		Police abuse/brutality	1
		Terrorism	2
		Religious extremism	3
		Inequality/Injustice	4
		Inter/intra community conflict	5
		Youth violence/gang	6
		Gender based violence	7
		Weak laws	8
		Non-enforcement of legal framework	9
		Others specify	
		_____	

D3 **Do more developed societies with greater respect for human rights have more effective government?**

Strongly agree	1
Agree	2
Neither agree nor disagree	3
Disagree	4
Strongly disagree	5

D4 **Most people in your country are not aware of the Universal Declaration of Human Rights?**

Strongly agree	1
Agree	2
Neither agree nor disagree	3
Disagree	4
Strongly disagree	5

D5 **How serious is the general human rights challenge in your country?**

Very serious	1
Serious	2
Less serious	3
Not serious at all	4

D6 **How free are you to practice any religion of your choice in your country?**

Very free	1
Free	2
Not free	3
Not free at all	4

D7	Law enforcement agencies in your country do not respect the rights of citizens?	
	Strongly agree	1
	Agree	2
	Neither agree nor disagree	3
	Disagree	4
	Strongly disagree	5

D8	Reinforcing the rights of women and girl child is very critical for sustainable development in your community/country?	
	Strongly agree	1
	Agree	2
	Neither agree nor disagree	3
	Disagree	4
	Strongly disagree	5

D9	Did the COVID-19 and state measures worsen the abuse of human rights in your community/country?	
	Yes	1
	No	2
	Indifference	3

D10	If yes to question 9 above, please state ways your rights was abused.

Section E: Humanitarian Pillars

Please tick ☑ the correct answer and also fill in the appropriate response by giving the necessary details in the spaces provided.

S/N	QUESTIONS	RESPONSES	CODE
E1	How do you rate the effectiveness of humanitarianism in your country?		
		Very effective	1
		Effective	2
		Ineffective	3
E2	Which risk is more prevalent in your country?		
		Human made risks	1
		Natural risk	2
E3	What are the threats to humanitarian pillars in your community/country?		
		Tick all that apply	
		Lack of early warning	1
		Lack of assistance to IDPs	2
		Natural disasters	3
		Man Made disasters	4
		Lack of protection for IDPs	5
		Food insecurity	6
		Ineffective disaster management	7
		Lack of preparedness & response	8

Lack of effective rehabilitation	9
Lack of assistance to victims	10
Others specify	

E4	Do humanitarian organisations in your country have the capacity and flexibility to adjust and adapt and work in synergy with other stakeholders?	
	Yes	1
	No	2
	Indifference	3

E5	What are the most unmet humanitarian needs of your country?	
	i.	
	ii.	
	iii.	
	iv.	

E6a	What roles do civil societies organisations play in humanitarian and development works in your country?

E6b	What roles does the private sector play in humanitarian and development works in your country?

E7	Humanitarian aids and support do not get to the people who need it in your country?	
	Strongly agree	1
	Agree	2
	Neither agree nor disagree	3
	Disagree	4
	Strongly disagree	5

E8	Rendering aids and help to the most vulnerable is also a humanitarian service?	
	Strongly agree	1
	Agree	2
	Neither agree nor disagree	3
	Disagree	4
	Strongly disagree	5

E9	Lack of good governance negatively affects humanitarian services in your country?	
	Strongly agree	1
	Agree	2
	Neither agree nor disagree	3
	Disagree	4
	Strongly disagree	5

E10 Targeting youth and women are critical in humanitarian services?

Strongly disagree	1
Agree	2
Neither agree nor disagree	3
Disagree	4
Strongly disagree	5

E11 Partiality negatively affects humanitarian services?

Strongly agree	1
Agree	2
Neither agree nor disagree	3
Disagree	4
Strongly disagree	5

E12 Lack of neutrality negatively affects humanitarian services?

Strongly agree	1
Agree	2
Neither agree nor disagree	3
Disagree	4
Strongly disagree	5

Section F: Interlink between the four pillars

Please tick ☑ the correct answer and also fill in the appropriate response by giving the necessary details in the spaces provided.

S/N	QUESTIONS	RESPONSES	CODE
F1	There is an interlink among peace and security, development, human rights and humanitarian?		
		Strongly agree	1
		Agree	2
		Neither agree nor disagree	3
		Disagree	4
		Strongly disagree	5
F2	Do you think technology affects the humanitarian, human rights, peace & security and development?		
		Yes	1
		No	2
		Indifference	3
F3	Do humanitarian and development actors work together in your community/country?		
		Yes	1
		No	2
		Indifference	3
F4	In what ways do human rights compliment peace and security and development?		

F5   **Are the effects of the threats to peace and security similar or the same with the effect of underdevelopment?**

Yes	1
No	2
Indifference	3

F6   **Lack of peace and security hinder development?**

Strongly agree	1
Agree	2
Neither agree nor disagree	3
Disagree	4
Strongly disagree	5

F7   **Underdevelopment is the cause and effect of human rights abuse in your country.**

Strongly agree	1
Agree	2
Neither agree nor disagree	3
Disagree	4
Strongly disagree	5

F8   **Addressing transboundary issues is critical in tackling conflict situations by harnessing the interlinkages?**

Strongly agree	1
Agree	2
Neither agree nor disagree	3
Disagree	4
Strongly disagree	5

F9   Human rights violations are the major cause of conflict in your country?

Yes	1
No	2
Indifference	3

F10a   Has your institution or organisation been utilizing methodologies and tools for integrating the four pillars into policies and practices.

Yes	1
No	2
Indifference	3

F10b   If yes, to question F10a, could you name them?

F11   Have there been opportunities in the application of the interlinkages approach for conflict prevention and resolution?

Yes	1
No	2
Indifference	3

F11a   If yes, to question F11, please mention them?

F12a   Have there been challenges in the application of the interlinkages approach for conflict prevention and resolution?

	Yes	1
	No	2
	Indifference	3

F12b **If yes, to question F12a, please mention them?**

F13 **Please comment on how you think that the four pillars could be harnessed or promote complementary interventions to contribute to effective lasting solutions to conflicts**

References

Aboidun, A. (2021). *#ENDSARS Panel Indicts Army, Police, Labels Lekki Tollgate Shooting 'A Massacre'.* Daily Trust. Retrieved January 6, 2022, from https://dailytrust.com/endsars-panel-indicts-army-police-labels-lekki-tollgate-shooting-a-massacre

(ALNAP), A. L. (2018). *Defining Humanitarian Aid.* 2016, T. W. (2016). *The World Humanitarian Summit 2016, Issue Paper May 2016.* The World Humanitarian Summit 2016, Issue Paper May 2016.

Agoha, C. (2012). Elite Leadership and Governance: The Triple Dilemma of Democratic Development in Nigeria. In S. Randranja, *African Power Elite: Identity, Domination and Accumulation. .* CODESIRA, Dakar.

Asunka, E.G.B. (2021 November 2). *Do Africans want democracy-and do they think they're getting it?* Retrieved from Afro Barometer: https://afrobarometer.org/blogs/do-africans-want-democracy-and-do-they-think-theyre-getting-it

Badejo, B. A. (1984). The Socio-Political Implications of Structural Adjustment Programme (SAP). *The Journal of Business and Social Studies, New Series, Vol. 7. No.1. .*

Badejo, B. A. (2019). Persistence of Corruption in Nigeria: Towards a Holistic Focus. In (. Sunday Bobai Agang et al, *A Multidimensional Perspective on Corruption in Africa: Wealth, Power, Religion and Democracy* (p. 141). Newcastle upon Tyne: Cambridge Scholars Publishing.

Badejo, B. A. (2020). *Peace and Security Operates Within a Quadruple Nexus. A Presentation at the International Peace Day Town Hall and Community Gathering.* Lagos: Yintab Strategy Consults.

Badejo, B. A. (2020). *Rethinking Security Initiatives in Nigeria.* Lagos: Yintab Books.

Badejo, B. A. (2020). The State of Anti-Corruption in Nigeria: 2015-2019. In P. P. Chris Jones, *Fighting Corruption in African Contexts: Our Collective Responsibility* (p. Chapter 2). Newcastle upon Tyne: Cambridge Scholars Publishing .

Badejo, B. A. (2021). *A Study Report on the Interlinkages Between the Development, Peace and Security, Human Rights and humanitarian Pillars in West and Central African Subregions.* United Nations Economic Commission for Africa.

Boutros-Ghali, B. (1995). An Agenda for Peace.

Daher, B. &. (2015). *Water-Energy-Food (WEF) Nexus Tool 2.0: Guiding Integrative Resources .*

Dittrich, M. G. (2012). *Economics around the World, The Role of Resources Use for the Development and the Environment.* Vienna and Heidelberg: Seri.

FAO. (2021). *The Federal Republic of Nigeria Resilience Strategy 2021-2023 Increasing the Resilience of Agriculture-Based Livelihood: The pathway to Humanitarian-Development-Peace Nexus.*

Francis, J. (2022). *CISLAC: Over 500,000 Lives lost to Armed Conflicts in Nigeria, according to Salaudeen Hashim, Programme Manager, Defence and Security, CISLAC.* New Telegraph.

Galtung, J. (1985). Twenty-five years of Peace Research: Ten Challenges and some Responses. *Journal of Peace Research.*

General, U. S. (2018). *Peacebuilding and Sustainable Peace, Report of UN SG.*

Gupta, S. D. (2000). *Corruption and Provision of Health Care and Education Services.* IMF Working Paper No. 116.

Guterres, A. (2016). *Secretary-General-designate Antonio Guterres' remarks to the General Assembly on taking the oath of office as Secretary-General, United Nations.* UN.

(2016). *High-Level Panel on Humanitarian Financing Report to the Secretary-General: Too important to fail - addressing the humanitarian financing gap. 2016.*

Horn, N. (2009). Human Rights Education in Africa. In A.B (eds),

   Human Rights in Africa: Legal perspectives on their protection and promotion.

How does War Damage the Environment?

International, T. (n.d.). *Annual Reports on Corruption Perception Index (CPI) Ranking.*

Jianguo Liu, V. H. (2018). *Nexus Approaches to Global Sustainable Development* . Nature Sustainability, Vol.1.

Kanife, E. (2021). *Nigerian Tech Startups are building the most exciting brands in Africa as they dominate the top 20 Challenger brands.* Technext.

Klarin, T. (2018). The Concept of Sustainable Development From its Beginning to Contemporary Issues. *Zagreb International Review of Economics and Business, Vol. 21, No.1,* 68.

Klarin, T. (2018). The Concept of Sustainable Development: From its Beginning to the Contemporary Issues. *Zagreb International Review of Economics and Business, Vol. 21, No.1,,* 68.

Maphosa, S. B. (2012). *Natural Resources and Conflict: Unlocking the Economic Dimension of Peace-Building in Africa. Policy Brief No.74.* African Institute of South Africa. .

Marian, V. (2014). *Democracy is often misunderstood with tragic results, says Stanford classicist.* . Stanford News.

Matters, L. S. (n.d.). *Report of Lekki Incident Investigation of 20th October, 2020.*

Murshed, M. (2018). *Impacts of Corruption on Sustainable Development: A Simultaneous Equations Model Estimation Approach.* ResearchGate.

Nations, U. (1987). *Report of the World Commission on Environment and Development "Our Common Future".*

Nations, U. (1987). *Report of the World Commission on Environment and Development "Our Common Future".*

Nations, U. *Transforming Our World: The 2030 Agenda for Sustainable Development. A/RES/70/1.*

NIAKATE, Z. M. (2011). Shared Governance of Peace and Security, The Malian Experience.

Obadan, M. I. (2006). *Overview of Exchange Rate Management in Nigeria from 1986 to date, Vol.30, No.3.*

Obaze, E. E. (2018). *Kofi Annan: In Service of the World.* Kujenga Amani Social Science Research Council. .

Obi, C. (2019). *Study on Strengthening and Mainstreaming the Peace, Development and Humanitarian Nexus into Policies and Strategies in Africa.*

Ochonu, M. (2020). *Liberal Democracy has Failed in Nigeria.* Africa is a Country .

Ochonu, M. (2021, October 1). The Democratic lie Story. (A. K. Newspaper, Interviewer)

OECD. (2013). *Government at a Glance 2013, Trust in Government, Policy Effectiveness and the Governance Agenda.*

OECD. (2019). *DAC Recommendation on the Humanitarian-Development-Peace Nexus.* .

Official, ECCAS. (2020, December 11). Interlinkages of peace and security, human rights, development and humanitarianism . (B. A. Badejo, Interviewer)

Pearce, D. (1989). *Tourism Development.* London: Harlow.

Planning, U. I. . *Public Expenditure Tracking Surveys in Education.*

Rasul, G. (2014). Food, water and energy security in South Asia: A Nexus Perspective from the Hindu Kush Himalayan Region. *Environment Science and Politics.39*, 35-48.

Reliefweb. (2021, september 22). *Web of Conflicts.* Retrieved from Reliefweb: https://reliefweb.int/report/nigeria/web-conflicts

Report, Pwc. (2017). *The Business of Entertainment, Harnessing Growth Opportunities in Entertainment, Media, Arts and Lifestyle* .

Ringler, C. B. (2013). The Nexus across Water, Energy, Land, and Food. (WELF): Potential for improved resource use efficiency. *Current Opinion Environmental Sustainability 5.*, 617-624.

Ross, A. &. (2016). The Evolution and Performance of River Basin Management in the Murray-Darling Basin. *Ecol.Soc. 21*, 39.

Sanni, K. (2021). *Boko Haram: 350,000 dead in Nigeria — UN.* Premium Times Nigeria. Retrieved January 6, 2022, from https://www.premiumtimesng.com/news/headlines/470476-insurgency-has-killed-almost-350000-in-north-east-undp.html

Sen, A. (1973). *Economic Inequality.* Oxford University Press.

Stanford Encyclopedia of Philosophy, Human Rights. (2003).

Tan, G. (2021). *Nigeria's Flutterwave in Talks to Triple Valuation to $3 Billion.* Bloomberg.

The Human Freedom Index.

Todaro, M. &. (2003). *Economic Development, (8th ed.).* Harlow: Pearson Education Limited .

Tschudin, A. (2021). *Presentation to the United Nations Office of the Special Adviser on Africa (OSAA), Strengthening the Capacity of African Countries to Design and Implement Policies that promote the Nexus between Peace, Humanitarian work, Development and Human Rights .*

UN, E. (2020). *Draft Report Virtual Inception Meeting on Subregional Studies on the Interlinkages Between the Development, Peace and Security, Human Rights, and Humanitarian Pillars .*

UNDP. (1994). *Human Development Report 1994. World Happiness Report.*

Index

About the Author

Babafemi A. Badejo, Nigerian, holds a Ph.D., (1982), in Political Science from the University of California, Los Angeles. He is a Solicitor and Advocate of the Supreme Court of Nigeria (1990), a Certified Mediator and Arbitrator. He is admitted unto the Lagos State Multi-Door Courthouse Panel of Neutrals.

He served as Senior Lecturer at the University of Lagos, before joining the United Nations for almost 24 years, holding senior level positions on peace operations, including as Deputy Special Representative of the UN Secretary-General for Somalia and Chief of Staff at two Missions, before his retirement in 2017.

A Consultant of repute who provided the framework for the Operationalization of the African Union Humanitarian Agency as well as the UN ECA Study on the Four-pillar Interlinkages for West and Central Africa.

He has provided advisory services to former Presidents of Nigeria, former President of East-Timor and Nobel Laureate, as well as the former President of the Court of the Prime Minister of the Kingdom of Bahrain as well as several former Special Representatives of the Secretary-General at several conflict hotspots in the Horn of Africa, East Africa and West Africa.

He is widely published on national and international political economy, conflict and peace as well as comparative political analysis. He is currently Professor of Political Science/International Relations at Chrisland University, Abeokuta, Nigeria.

www.ingramcontent.com/pod-product-compliance
Lightning Source LLC
Chambersburg PA
CBHW050610280326
41932CB00016B/2979